Pass The Test

An Employee Guide To Drug Testing

Beverly A. Potter, Ph.D.
J. Sebastian Orfali, M.A.

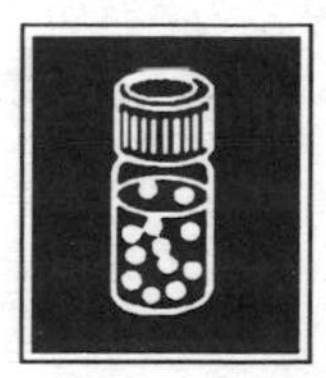

RONIN Publishing, Inc.
PO Box 522, Berkeley, CA 94701
www.roninpub.com

Published by
Ronin Publishing, Inc.
Post Office Box 522
Berkeley, CA 94701
www.roninpub.com

Pass The Test
An Employee Guide To Drug Testing
ISBN: 1-57951-008-6

NOTE: Portions of material in this book were published under the title, *Drug Testing At Work: A Guide For Employers And Employees*, and was copyright ® 1990, 1995, by Beverly Potter & Sebastian Orfali.

Printed in the USA
Distributed by Publishers Group West

9 8 7 6 5 4 3 2 1

Cover design: Judy July, Generic Typography
Design & layout: Beverly Potter
Copy editing: Steve Cook

Acknowledgements

We are grateful to the many people who helped in researching, writing, editing and producing this book. We especially appreciate the companies who gave us information about their services and products. A special thanks to Mark Hart of Hewlett-Packard and Kathy Deines of PharmChem Laboratories for the invaluable information they provided.

Also by Dr. Beverly Potter

Drug Testing At Work
A Guide For Employers

Overcoming Job Burnout
How To Renew Enthusiasm For Work

Preventing Job Burnout
A Workbook

The Worrywart's Companion
21 Ways To Soothe Yourself & Worry Smart

From Conflict To Cooperation
How To Mediate A Dispute

The Way Of The Ronin
Riding The Waves Of Change At Work

Brain Boosters
Foods & Drugs That Make You Smarter

The Healing Magic Of Cannabis

Turning Around
Keys To Motivation & Productivity

Also by J. Sebastian Orfali

Drug Testing At Work
A Guide For Employers

Brain Boosters
Foods & Drugs That Make You Smarter

Computer Comics

Author Strategies
How To Create A Book Proposal That Sells!
(audio cassette)

Table Of Contents

NOTE TO READER:

The material herein is presented for reference and informational purposes, not as legal advice. Furthermore, certain practices described in this book are illegal. The authors and publisher do not support breaking the law. Certain illegal practices described in this book are for information. Readers are encouraged to consult an attorney for specific legal advice about these practices. Additionally, drug testing laws are constantly changing and can vary from state-to-state. The material in this book is generalized. Readers should search out specific information tailored to their specific situation.

CHAPTER 1

Birth Of The Drug-Free Workplace

The end of the "Me-generation" in 1979 was marked by an unprecedented high level of self-medicating and recreational drug use. In reaction, President Reagan tried to put the reins on drugs with the Executive Order 12564 in 1986 calling for a "drug-free workplace," which made it a condition of employment for all Federal employees to refrain from using drugs. All Federal agencies were ordered to develop a comprehensive drug-free workplace program. Reagan insisted that it was not a punitive measure and promised people would not be fired or otherwise hurt. He promised that people discovered to be drug users would receive help.

Of course, the Office of Personnel Management's regulations did not adhere to Reagan's promises that Federal workers found to be drug users would not be fired. As it turned out, employees could be fired for a single incidence of illegal drug use and dismissal for a second offense was required. Worse, the agencies did not have to demonstrate that the drug use affected the employee's work. Furthermore, the definition of "sensitive" position was so broad that more than half of all

Federal workers were included. Under the regulations, disciplinary action, which could include a written reprimand, putting the employee on leave, suspending or firing the employee, was required to be taken against Federal workers after a single confirmed positive drug test, and those who refused to take the test could be fired for "failing to meet a condition of employment".

So much for Big Brother's promises. Are you surprised?

The Drug-Free Workplace Act Of 1988

Next came the Drug-Free Workplace Act of 1988 which tightened up Reagan's Executive Order. This law requires Federal grantees and contractors having a contract for property or services of $25,000 or more to provide a drug free workplace. It was the first extension of Federal antidrug legislation into the workplace of Federal contractors and grantees. While drug testing isn't a requirement of the Drug-Free Workplace Act, drug testing demonstrates compliance with the legislation and is the generally accepted standard.

National Drug Control Strategy

Broadcast from the Oval Office in 1989, President Bush unveiled on primetime TV the first National Drug Control Strategy—a comprehensive blueprint for controlling drug use and sales. Bush defended drug testing at work, despite widespread charges that it is an invasion of privacy and test results are often inaccurate.

Each year since, the National Drug Control Strategy has been reviewed and ratcheted up, becoming more punitive and force-based. With each tightening comes another inroad into our freedom. The majority of spending is devoted towards law enforcement, which involves arresting and imprisoning drug offenders. Only about 30% of the budget is allocated to treatment, prevention and research. Treatment is usually coercive, and prevention is mostly prohibitionist propaganda.

In 1998, amid much fanfare, President Clinton brought forth the latest rendition which this time outlines a "ten-year plan", with the emphasis on saving the Nation's youth from drugs. Of course, it was widely applauded. After all, who is in favor of youths ruining their lives with drugs? What was overlooked is that in 1998, drug use had hit an all time low since its 1979 historic high level. No matter. Clinton increased the budget for the war on drugs to an all time high and called for 100,000 more police to fight drugs.

Interestingly, and not too surprisingly, the illicit drug used most widely is marijuana and most positive drug tests are for marijuana. In the late 1990s medical marijuana gained growing acceptance and was legalized in California and Arizona. Clinton's drug control strategy included countering attempts to legalize marijuana. The Federal government's response to these voter approved initiatives was to bring charges against the "buyers' clubs" which distributed "medical" marijuana to members with serious ailments. It became something of a standoff between states and cities against Big Brother. Oakland, California was so supportive of The Oakland Cannabis Buyers' Club—which required a doctor's prescription to belong—that the city council deputized the Club's staff in an attempt to render them immune from Federal prosecution.

In addition to widespread growing sympathy for medical marijuana, "hempsters" gained support for hemp and hemp products. George Washington grew hemp, they proclaimed, and used pot to soothe his toothaches and inflamed gums. Clearly threatened, the government said, "Permitting hemp cultivation would result in *de facto* legalization of marijuana cultivation because both hemp and marijuana come from the same plant—*Cannabis sativa.* Chemical analysis is the only way to differentiate between cannabis variants intended for hemp production and hybrids grown for psychoactive properties."

If pot were legalized, drug abuse statistics would drop by more than 50%. Then what would happen to the budget for the war on drugs and all of the law enforcement agencies that feed upon it?

Omnibus Transportation Employee Testing Act

In 1991 the Department of Transportation (DOT) adopted mandatory rules requiring private employers in the transportation industry, which includes aviation, railroad and transit companies, to adopt substance-abuse prevention programs, including drug and alcohol testing. This stringent law specifies each step in the drug testing process, including how a person is asked to remove clothing by the collection site person, how much urine constitutes a sample, use of split samples, testing the sample for temperature within 4 minutes, which tests can be used for screening and which for confirmation, and so forth. It includes required drug testing for operators of commercial motor vehicles from Canada and Mexico. These rules also include specific procedures for testing for alcohol.

The Omnibus Transportation Act brought an additional eight million safety-sensitive employees under Federal regulation, making DOT the overseer of the Nation's largest workplace drug testing program. Transportation companies are expected to test applicants before they are hired, randomly, following accidents, when there is reasonable suspicion that an employee is abusing drugs or alcohol and when past violators return to performing safety-sensitive jobs, called "post-positive follow-up" testing.

If you're a transportation worker and test positive, DOT requires your company to refer you to a substance-abuse professional before returning to work. If substance abuse is diagnosed, you must receive treatment before resuming duties.

The Omnibus Transportation Bill was so successful that in 1998 both the Federal Highway Administration (FHWA) and the Federal Aviation Administration (FAA) lowered the minimum annual random alcohol-testing rate from 25 percent to 10 percent for commercial drivers and aviation industry employees.

Conflicting State Laws

In addition to Federal drug testing mandates, each state has its own laws for handling alcohol and drug abuse in the workplace which vary dramatically from state to state. For example, twelve states—Alaska, California, Colorado, Connecticut, Iowa, Maine, Massachusetts, Minnesota, Montana, New Jersey, New York, Rhode Island, Vermont and West Virginia—and two cities ban, or significantly restrict random testing. Onsite testing is similarly regulated by state laws. In some cases, states limit company options in handling initial on-site positive tests, while other states outlaw on-site testing altogether.

By 1998, several states had begun to restrict hair-testing. To complicate matters, each year there are new state laws and more precedent setting court cases. The Institute for a Drug-Free Workplace in Washington DC catalogs the State and Federal drug-testing laws, court cases and arbitration outcomes into a helpful publication called *Guide to State and Federal Drug-Testing Laws.* This publication is expensive and not readily available. However, if you request it, your local library or your company library will probably purchase it for their collection.

CHAPTER 2

Reasons For Drug Testing

There are many reasons why your company would want to test you for drugs. Maybe you may have been involved in an accident. Maybe they want to find out if you have been using drugs. Sometimes drug testing is used to determine if you're fit to work. Other times your company's objective is to deter you and your co-workers from using drugs, in which case random testing will be used. Drug testing of job applicants is common.

"Presumptive" testing is used when a supervisor, for example, observes an unkempt appearance, slurred speech or other indications of intoxication and suspects you have been using drugs. Proof of abstinence is another reason for testing and is commonly used as an adjunct to drug abuse treatment. If you've tested positive, giving regular drug-free urines can be a condition of keeping your job. Less commonly you might ask to be tested to prove that you have been drug-free—to demonstrate that you were not at fault in the case of an accident, for example.

Investigating Accidents

Testing for drugs is very common following an industrial accident. You face two risks in post-accident testing. For example, if you have been receiving medication under doctor's prescription, that medication or its metabolites will probably appear in your urine, and illicit drug use may be inferred. Second, drug metabolites can be detected in your urine long after any intoxication or impairment. This could occur with some medications, or if you smoked marijuana a few days before, but not the day of, the accident. In this situation the presence of cannabinoids in your urine can be construed as proof that you were stoned at the time of the accident. So while post-accident testing sounds reasonable on the face of it, the data yielded may not actually be relevant to the accident in question. Unfortunately, many employers don't understand this which means you could find yourself being held responsible for an accident you didn't cause, as an example of one of many awful possibilities.

Work Fitness

Testing for drug use may be used to determine if you are fit to work. For example, if you are an airline pilot you might have to blow into a breathalyzer, which records alcohol vapor on the flight recorder, before assuming flight command. If measurable levels of alcohol are present, it will be displayed to you and your crew members.

Mass Screening

The word "screen" refers to an inexpensive, easy-to-analyze test administered to a large number of people with the purpose of catching drug users. Screening tests are used prior to employment and in random testing. The military and many corporations randomly screen employees to detect drug users. Personnel to be screened are selected at random, without any reason to suspect drug use. People included in mass screenings can be pulled from all positions and levels of the organization and not solely from high risk, safety or security jobs.

Experts and officials argue that random testing is the most effective deterrent to drug use because everyone in the company has some chance of being tested on any given day. Drug testing proponents argue that random testing is fair because there is no stigma or accusation attached because you've been selected at random. And random testing is supposedly not influenced by supervisor biases.

Civil rights attorneys reject these arguments. They say that random testing "reverses the presumption of innocence upon which much of our jurisprudence is built, and violates the strong prohibition of dragnet searches sweeping in the many who are innocent in order to find the few who are guilty which is the hallmark of a free and democratic society." Basically, random drug testing is a fishing trip. People who are completely drug free can and do get caught. You want to make sure you're not one of them!

Mass screening programs are responsible for most of the false positives and have drawn the most criticism. Even though you may have no history of drug use you are treated with suspicion. Furthermore, if you have used prescription drugs and over-the-counter drugs you can test positive. Then you must defend yourself to prove your innocence. Even if you don't come up positive, you never know what else they might be finding out from your bodily fluids, such as being pregnant or having a medical condition, that you just as soon not have your boss know about.

Pre-Employment Screening

Screening urine of job applicants to detect drug use in order to avoid hiring drug users is a common purpose of drug testing. You could be denied a job even though you only occasionally use drugs off the job with no resultant work impairment, or don't use drugs at all. If you are looking for work it behooves you to learn everything you can about drug testing and to be proactive—even if you are completely drug free—in preparing for the test so that you can pass and get the job, earn a living, and make your unique contribution to society. Companies don't usually tell you why they've not hired you. You may get a positive drug test and never know it or be given the opportunity to clear yourself.

Presumptive Testing

A "presumptive" situation is one in which there is some strong reason to suspect—or presume—you have been using drugs. A test is administered to detect or confirm the presumption. For example, your supervisor might notice that you smell of alcohol and walk with a staggering gait; or you might show signs of sedative use such as lethargy. So your supervisor would request drug testing.

You can imagine how this could be abused. In one case, a man had a cold and was in a bad mood because of an argument with his wife. His supervisor noted that he was sniffling and seemed distracted and ordered him tested. Presumptive testing, sometimes called "probable cause" testing, is also used after accidents.

To Confirm A Positive Result

Confirmatory tests are used to check the results of the initial or screening test. Samples that test positive are retested or "confirmed" with a more powerful and accurate testing method which is more expensive and yields fewer false positives.

Whether or not a confirmation is conducted depends on the intended use of the results. If you are being tested as part of a drug treatment program, where the goal is detection of early relapse and a positive result has no disciplinary consequences, screening methods alone are adequate and confirmation of a particular sample is not needed. On the other hand, in situations in which a single positive urine test could result in discipline, termination of employment, or loss of professional license, "forensic" or legal standards of testing positives using a different confirmatory method are essential. And you should demand no less.

Generally, a second urine sample is not taken for confirmatory testing. Instead a portion of your urine sample is preserved and used for the confirmatory test. The important thing is that a chemically different and more powerful test is used to confirm the initial positive result.

Controlling Abuse

The Federal government demands that drug testing be used to control drug use. The military, for example, does not do pre-enlistment testing. They will take you as a drug user because they expect to clean you up and make you into a fighting machine. The military uses random testing extensively to scare you into abstinence because otherwise you can face court-martial and possible dishonorable discharge, which will follow you around for the rest of your life. The fact is, it works. When the Navy introduced random testing positive tests dropped from 48 percent in 1980 to 21 percent in 1982. Once again, marijuana was the most common drug detected. Ignored is the notable shift to increased alcohol use. So our GI's are getting drunk and destroying their livers instead of getting high and expanding their minds!

Proponents of testing argue that using drug testing to control drug use is legitimate, because when random testing is implemented and people expect to be tested, only drug abusers will get positive results. Of course, this is not true. Lots of innocent people test positive and are accused of being drug abusers.

Proof Of Abstinence

Drug testing can be used to prove that you have been drug-free. For example, if you were an anesthesiologist recovering from chemical dependency, you might give a urine specimen following any operation with anesthetic complications. If a lawsuit were filed and the plaintiff's attorney discovered the your history of drug abuse, the attorney would probably claim that the mishap occurred because the anesthesiologist was intoxicated. A negative drug test result helps document that the complication was not caused by your having used drugs. Such documentation can provide substantial legal protection for both you and the hospital as well.

As An Adjunct To Treatment

If you've tested positive and have entered a rehabilitation program as a result, you will probably be expected to provide urine for regular testing as a condition of treatment. Such testing is considered a valuable adjunct to treatment. Drug users often imagine they can return to controlled use of drugs which testing can detect. Regular testing can help you to break a drug habit. Most treatment professionals believe drug testing is a positive tool for monitoring recovery of the chemically dependent.

CHAPTER 3

What Is Tested

Several different kinds of bodily materials can be tested for drugs, and their reliability can range from excellent to nil, depending on what is being tested and what kind of tests are performed upon it. The materials most often used in drug testing are urine, hair, breath, saliva, sweat, and blood. Additionally, certain behavioral and psychological cues are sometimes interpreted as evidence of drug abuse.

Metabolites And Metabolism

After a drug is swallowed, smoked, injected, or snorted, it is distributed throughout the bloodstream. As the blood repeatedly passes through the liver and other parts of the body, the drug encounters numerous enzyme systems, which convert it into one or more end products called metabolites which travel into various parts of the body, including urine, blood, and hair. Your individual metabolism determine how long such a process would take in your body. "Detection time" is the length of time the metabolites stay detectable in the body.

Urine

Urine is usually tested because of the ease of getting a sample, the speed of conducting the analysis, and the low cost. Urine tests can show the presence of drug metabolites or physiological by-products. The major problem of testing urine is that presence of drug metabolites in urine is treated as proof that you were under the influence of the drug at the time the sample was given. This is not the case at all. At best it reveals *recent* drug use. But by the time that metabolities make it into your urine you are no longer stoned and the drug is not actively affecting your functioning. This is particularly true with marijuana which can lead to positive test results two or three weeks or longer after use.

Drug Urinalysis

Urine drug screening is an analytical tool for detecting the presence of drugs and their metabolites in urine. The technology for performing urinalysis varies, and can be designed to meet the specific needs of individual employers.

The major limitation of urinary drug tests is their lack of specificity, unless a GC/MS (gas chromatography/mass spectrometry) test is performed. It is harder to determine with a urine test than with a blood test when a drug was taken. There is considerable individual variability in detection times. Diet, urine flow, and dose dependency can alter the test results. Furthermore some people test positive at lower doses than others.

Breath

Breath testing is commonly used by police to test motorists for alcohol. It has the advantage of being nonintrusive, inexpensive, and almost instantaneous. A positive breath test indicates a high percent of alcohol in the blood, which is a positive indication of intoxication.

Disposable breath analyzers for motorists, used by drivers to determine before driving if they've had DUIs, have become a competitive business. Before driving you exhale into a tube filled with yellow crystals, and the crystals turn blue-green if you're too drunk to drive, according to legal standards. Many breath testing products are for sale to the general public and can be found on the Internet.

New rules for alcohol testing went into effect in 1995-96 which increased the use of breath analysis. It is required at collection sites with the use of "evidential breath testing" (EBT)—a device that costs between $2000-$8000 and requires a specially trained technician.

Saliva

Testing saliva for marijuana can presumably determine recent use, whereas use of marijuana weeks in the past can sometimes cause a positive urine test in regular users. Intravenously administered tetrahydrocannabinol (THC), the primary psychoactive ingredient in marijuana, does not appear in significant amounts in human saliva, which means that cannabinoids detected in saliva result from recent smoking or oral ingestion. Because THC metabolites can be detected in urine several days and sometimes weeks after marijuana has been smoked, a saliva test is considered to be a useful alternative to document recent marijuana use, which can be detected up to 10 hours after smoking a single joint.

Blood

Blood testing measures the actual presence of the drug or its metabolite in the blood at the time of testing. Blood-test results are therefore the most accurate indicator of intoxication. However, blood testing is used infrequently because it requires trained medical skill and specialized equipment, which makes it expensive.

If you were involved in an accident and know that you were drug and alcohol free, you could request that a blood sample be collected at same time as giving your urine sample. Then if you get a positive result on the urine, you can request that the blood be analyzed to prove you were not intoxicated at the time of the accident. It is important that your sample be frozen, since drug metabolites deteriorate.

Depending on the dose, marijuana can be easily detected by testing blood up to six hours after consumption. After that, concentration falls rapidly, and marijuana is not generally detectable in blood after 22 hours.

Hair

As hair grows drugs and their metabolites are absorbed into its structure. Once a metabolite is embedded in the sheath of the hair, a longitudinal record of drug use is created. Metabolites appear in detectable levels in hair about a week after drug use. Because hair grows about 1/4 to 1/2 inch a month, the shaft can be cut into lengths creating a sort of time line of drug use.

National Institute of Justice Research showed that at low levels of cocaine use, the radioimmunoassay of hair (RIAH) detects about 10 times as many drug users at current accepted cut-off levels than does urine analysis; while at moderate levels of cocaine use, the RIAH detects 3 to 4 times as many users as does urinalysis. Hair analysis does not pick up single or very infrequent drug use, however.

The Danger In Testing Hair

Hair testing uses the same technologies as testing urine for drugs; the difference is in what is being tested, urine or hair. Hair analysis is especially threatening to our personal freedom as compared to other drug testing methods. Hair retains drug components for longer periods, and drug use can be detected in hair for weeks or even months compared to the 2 to 3 days that cocaine or heroin can be detected in blood or urine. Furthermore, hair specimens can be readily obtained without the privacy problems encountered with urine or the invasiveness of drawing blood. Since hair testing is less invasive it is likely to be given greater latitude by the Courts.

Since drug testing has become a fact of life, a lot of strategies have developed for passing the test. Hair testing threatens to change all the rules. For one thing, hair expands the window for detection of all illicit drugs. Whereas urine testing can detect drug use for several days to a week or two, hair testing detects presence of drugs for several months—or more with long hair. Worse yet, for recreational drug users who want to keep their jobs—brief periods of abstinence cannot be used to clean up long enough to pass the test.

Another worry is that hair is easy to handle and because it is inert it does not require special storage conditions. Hair lends itself to repeat testing because collecting comparable samples is quite easy. Finally, while urine samples can be adulterated in a variety of ways; it is practically impossible to foil hair analysis. In fact, hair analysis can be conducted on deceased people years after they've died, which is impossible with urine and blood testing. Dr. Ron Siegel of UCLA, for example, analyzed strands of hair of John Keats, the nineteenth-century Romantic English poet, and proved that Keats was, indeed, an opium smoker.

In the 1960's you could tell a doper by his long hair. As we move into the era of hair testing that may all change and we may see more dopers who shave their heads—along with their eyebrows, legs, armpits, chest and pubic hair! Remember, the longer, the hair the longer the record.

Problems With Hair Testing

Drugs bind into hair at different rates depending upon the hair. African-Amercians' hair has been demonstrated to absorb drug metabolities at rates 10 to 50 times greater than the hair of Caucasians, which can influence the likelihood of a positive drug test. Another problem is that hair absorbs contaminants from the air. When you are exposed to drug smoke, metabolites are absorbed into your hair and can cause a positive test result. This problem is particularly acute with marijuana because the lipophilic or fat soluble components of THC readily binds into the structure of human hair.

So if your old man (or old lady!), for example, has been smoking dope around you, especially in a small confined place, like a car or in the bedroom, you can be sure that it has been absorbed into your hair. If your hair is tested, you can get a positive. The longer your hair, the longer the record.

Sweat

Sweat is a sensitive indicator of heroin and cocaine use. Usually urine is used in testing but it has the drawback that most drugs are cleared from urine in 2 to 3 days after use. In order to effectively monitor drug use on a continuing basis urine screening would have to be performed 2 to 3 times a week.

Drug metabolites are excreted into sweat which can be collected over several days or weeks by small patches worn on the skin. Sweat testing is now being performed for cocaine, amphetamines, and opiates.

The PharmChek® Drugs of Abuse Patch

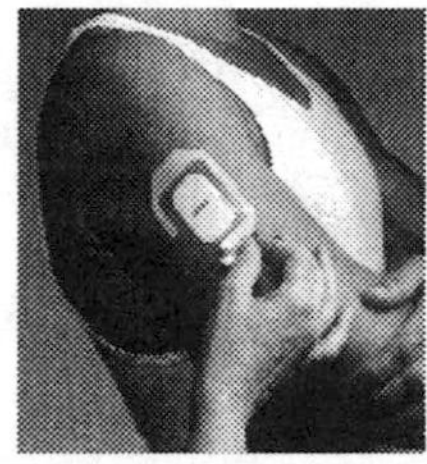
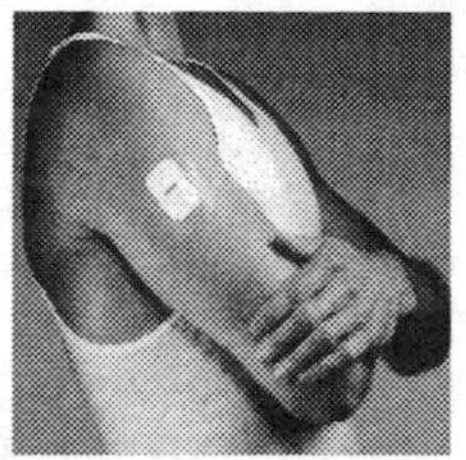
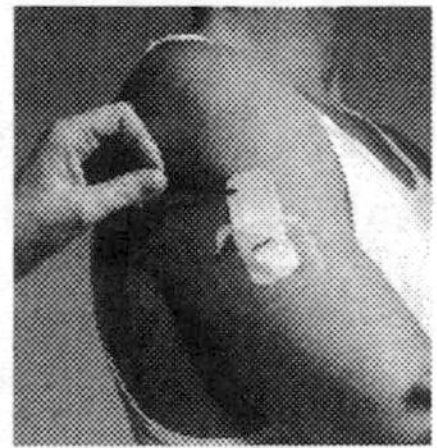

The "sweat patch" from PharmChem can be applied to the upper, outer arm or the lower midriff. After it has been worn, the absorption pad is removed from the sweat patch and sent to the laboratory for analysis. (Photo courtesy of PharmChem, Menlo Park, CA.)

The sweat patch is a useful monitoring device for people in drug abuse treatment or under court supervision or on probation. The patch is designed so that once removed, it cannot be reattached to the skin, which prevents tampering. Patches can be frozen until subjected to testing. Sweat testing is still in the developmental stages. Assays and cut-offs levels have not been determined.

The concept of wearing a patch to collect sweat for analysis is a bit daunting. Perhaps we'll soon have to put on a sweat-collecting bracelet when we punch the time clock so that our fluids can be subjected to continuous monitoring.

CHAPTER 4

Testing Methods

Drug testing methods vary greatly in their cost, accuracy, time required for analysis, selectivity, and sensitivity. Typically, laboratories use a low-cost screening procedure first, then check positive results with a more expensive more accurate method. The most popular screening methods are immunochemical tests called *immunoassays* and *thin-layer chromatography* (TLC).

Immunoassays

The immunoassay is a screening method that yields a "yes or no" result with a high degree of sensitivity and specificity The most commonly used immunoassays are enzyme immunoassay (EIA), radioimmunoassay (RIA), and fluorescence polarization immunoassay (FPIA). All three tests work on the same basic principle that utilizes binding antibodies capable of recognizing drugs or drug groups. When urine or hair extract containing a drug is mixed in solution with the drug's antibody, it binds to the antibody.

The basic principle is similar to that of the "rabbit test" for pregnancy. Drugs to be detected are coupled to large molecules and injected into rabbits or sheep. The animal's immune system produces antibodies against the specific drug. These antibodies are then purified for use in immunoassay tests. Competition occurs for available antibody binding sites between the tagged drug in the test and the drug in the unknown sample.

Limitations

Immunoassay tests can discriminate only between the presence and absence of the suspected drug, so they yield only an estimate of the quantity of drug in your system. Cross-reactivity, in which non-drug substances and over-the-counter drugs bind with the antibodies, is a serious shortcoming of this method and can cause a false positive—a positive for a drug metabolite not actually present in the urine.

Cross-Reactivity And Specificity

The specificity of an immunoassay refers to the antibody to recognizing only the drug or drug group in question. "Cross-reactivity", on the other hand, is the tendency of antibodies to recognize substances other than the drug being tested for. In other words, an antibody that has high specificity will be low in cross-reactivity. The degree of cross-reactivity varies widely among immunoassays. Although all three techniques are considered highly specific relative to other screening methods, they are not infallible. Immunoassays for amphetamines, for example, will react with drugs structurally related to the amphetamines, such as the over-the-counter sympathomimetic amines, phenylpropanolamine and ephedrine. For this reason, confirmation of positive immunochemical results by a fundamentally different chemical technique such as GC/MS is a necessity. Unfortunately, this doesn't always happen. Instead, the test may be confirmed with the same or similar test used previously or it may not be confirmed at all.

Enzyme Immunoassay

The EIA assay uses an enzyme to label the drug present in the sample. When bound to the antibody, this enzyme is inactive and becomes activated as it is displaced from antibody binding sites by drugs present in the specimen. The degree to which this reaction occurs is proportional to the amount of drug present.

The Enzyme Multiplied Immunoassay Test (EMIT®) manufactured by Syva Corporation in Palo Alto relies on modifying an enzyme's ability to act on its substrate, lysozyme. An animal is injected with the drug or a drug metabolite, usually in combination with other chemicals. The injection provokes the animal to produce specific immune chemicals, called antigens, that will bind to the drug. These antigens are then harvested by extracting and purifying certain proteins (gamma globulins) from the animal's blood. The lysozymes or other enzymes are bound to the drug or metabolite of interest, such as morphine, amphetamine, or methadone. This drug-enzyme complex is inactivated as a functional enzyme when the drug antibody is placed in the same solution. If, however, an urine sample contains the drug in question, the antibody will bind less of the drug-enzyme complex, because the antibody will also bind to the free drug. Any unbound drug enzyme is active and loses the substrate bacterial suspension, clearing the solution. This clearing is measured as a change in absorption of light by using special testing instrument called a spectrophotometer.

The Radioimmunoassay

Abuscreen® is a popular radioimmunoassay manufactured by Hoffman-LaRoche. It uses technology similar to the EMIT® test. The RIA also uses specially produced antibodies, but differs from the EMIT® by using radioactive isotopes, called tracers, to label and measure the results. The amount of the tracer that displaces drugs bound to the antibody indicates the concentration of the drug present. Radiation emitted by the antibody bound tracer is measured using a gamma counter.

RIA is considered more accurate than EMIT®, but is somewhat more costly and requires more sophisticated laboratories due to the use of radioactive isotopes. Since EMIT® and RIA are both immunoassay techniques, one should not be used as a back-up or confirming test for the other. Instead, a positive test result should be confirmed by a nonimmunological procedure such as gas chromatography.

The most important weakness of immunoassays generally is their lack of specificity, because there are few antisera that are specific for a single compound. A more sensitive and more specific technique, fluorescent polarization immunoassy (FPIA) was developed by Abbott Labs and extended to testing drugs of abuse in 1986.

Confirmatory Tests

A positive result on a screening test should not taken at face value. It must be confirmed by a second more powerful test that is based upon a different chemical principle.

Gas Chromatography

Gas Chromatography (GC) and Gas Liquid Chromatography (GLC) are testing methods that separate molecules by use of a glass or metal tube packed with material of a particular polarity.

The sample to be tested is vaporized at the injection port, and carried through the column by a steady flow of gas. Identical compounds travel through the column at the same speed, since their interaction with the column packing is identical. The column terminates at a detector that permits recording and quantification. The time from injection until a response is observed at the recorder is referred to as the "retention time."

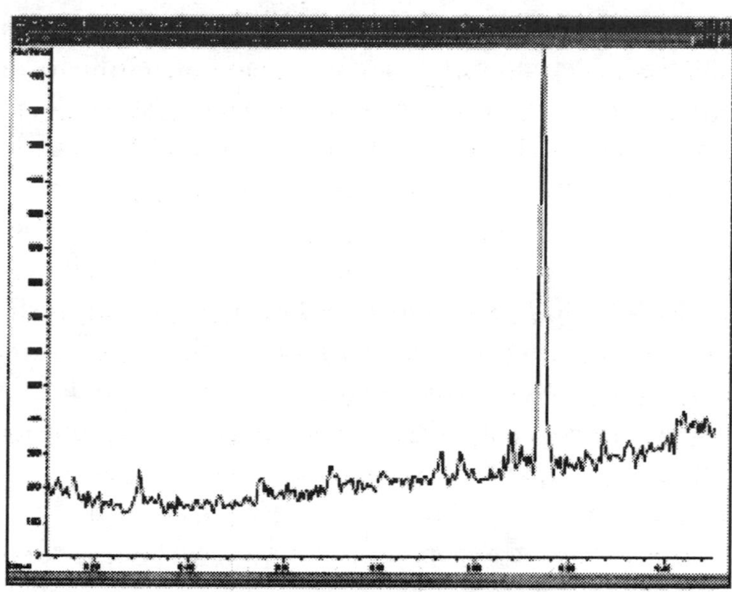

Chromatogram for THC-OTBDMS

Identical retention time of substances running on the same column is strong evidence that the substances are identical. The GC, as well as other testing methods, require the use of standards of reference materials to calibrate the tests.

Gas Chromatography/Mass Spectrometry

Confirmatory tests should be done with gas chromatography/mass spectrometry, which is the state-of-the-art technique in analytical toxicology. It combines two analytical techniques: gas chromatography and mass spectrometry. The reason to do a confirmatory test is to double check for human error. Gas chromatography with a mass spectrometry detector (GC/MS) is the most sensitive and specific procedure commonly used for drug identification. Because of its cost and the sophisticated skills needed to do the analysis, it is used primarily for confirmatory tests and for tests that must meet forensic courtroom standards.

GC/MS technique can be used both quantitatively and qualitatively. Depending on the drug measured, sensitivity can be measured between nanograms and picograms. GC/MS is more specific and 100 to 1,000 times more sensitive than the TLC system. Most organic molecules, including commonly used drugs such as marijuana, cocaine, and heroin, are readily identified.

GC/MS, GLC, and some RIA methodologies can be applied effectively to all biological fluids, including serum or blood. Blood levels of drugs are important because only these levels indicate *actual levels of intoxication*, a fact that could have great legal significance.

GC/MS mixes a urine or hair specimen with an organic solvent. The organic solvent is then evaporated to concentrate the drug prior to introduction into the GC/MS. The technique consists of two steps. First is the separation of drugs in a gas chromatograph followed by mass spectrometry of the separated drug(s).

Gas chromatography forces a gas, usually helium, through a thin fused silica column with a crosslinked silicone polymer layer. Vaporized drugs are separated by interaction with the polymer and arrive at the end of the column separated in time, known as "retention time (RT)".

The sample is first separated into components by gas chromatography, and then mass spectrometry is used to identify the substances emerging from the gas chromatograph. The mass spectrometer subjects the components to an electron beam that breaks them into fragments and accelerates them through a magnetic field. A molecule of a drug always breaks into the same fragments, known as its mass spectrum. A mass spectrum for each drug is unique, like a fingerprint. Information on the fragmentation pattern is compared to a computer library, which lists that mass of the parent compound and its most likely fragments. A 98 percent match is considered confirmation of the presence of the compound.

Detection by GC/MS is highly specific, but the equipment for GC/MS is costly, and great technical expertise is required to interpret the analysis of the results. GC/MS devices provide state-of-the-art accuracy and are widely used in forensic, pharmaceutical, clinical, and industrial service laboratories.

In the second step, the capillary fused silica column is inserted into the mass spectrometer device which consists of a high vacuum chamber with quadropoles surrounding the end of the gas chromatograph column. Drugs are ionized by electrons as they exit the column and are forced into the quadropoles separating the fragments on the basis of their electrical charge and molecular weights. An ion detector converts the charged fragments into electrical pulses and feeds the information into a dedicated computer. Resultant mass spectra are extremely characteristic of the original molecule.

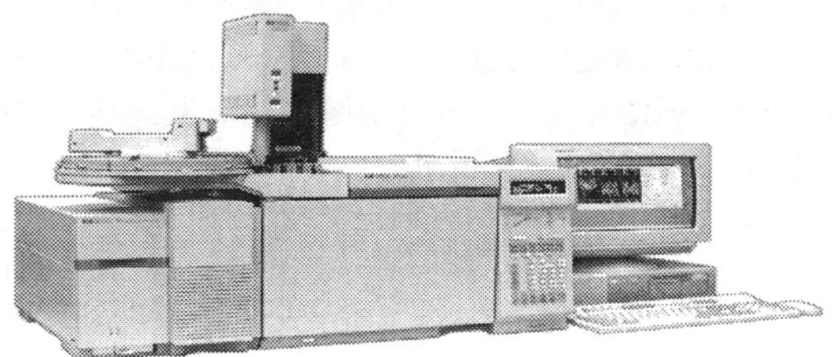

The Hewlett-Packard Mass Selective Detector (Courtsey of Hewlett-Packard, Palo Alto, CA.)

The GC/MS had been out of the reach of most laboratories because of the cost and the technical expertise needed. However, advances in computerization, automated samples, and analytic technology have now placed GC/MS capability within the reach of most labs because costs have come down and testing is more automated. Many labs use the Hewlett-

Packard Mass Selective Detector connected to a Hewlett-Packard gas chromatograph. The GC/MS is highly reliable—provided the operator is adequately trained and performing competently.

Thin-Layer Chromatography

Thin-Layer Chromatography, or TLC, is a form of chromatography that is used less frequently in the 1990s than formerly. It is included here because readers may still come across references to TLC. As in other chromatography, the urine is extracted with a reagent, and the extract is then subjected to a procedure that causes the components to separate. With thin-layer chromatography (TLC), results are created by the reproducible migration pattern of a drug on a thin layer of absorbant, usually a silica-coated glass plate. The plate is sprayed with a solution that reacts differently with different drugs, producing colored spots, that represent different drugs.

The sample is "spotted" by putting a drop of urine extract on the TLC plate that is put in a solvent which runs up the plate by capillary action, carrying with it the drugs present in the extract. A specific drug will always migrate to the same spot or spots. After drying, the plate is analyzed for the position of drugs of interest. If cocaine is present in the sample, for example, the visualization solution is sprayed and reveals a specific spot on the plate that indicates where the cocaine has traveled. The spot location is identified by an "Rf" number which is a ratio of the distance traveled by the drug in question to the distance traveled by the solvent from the origin, where the sample was originally spotted. The plate can be illuminated by ultraviolet lights. Identical molecules are expected to migrate to the same Rf zone and to give identical color reactions. TLC often produces false positives in which certain over-the-counter and prescription drugs will travel to approximately the same spot in the testing device as illegal substances. Therefore, re sults of TLC must be interpreted by a skilled technician and positive results must be confirmed by a more reliable testing method.

TLC has been used most often in drug detoxification clinics, methadone maintenance programs, testing of parolees and prison inmates, and industrial screening.

Problems With TLC Tests

Results from thin-layer chromography tests are qualitative, giving either a positive or negative result. Positive results cannot be quantified. While this is also true of the immunoassay tests, using several tests with different cut-off valves can yield a somewhat quantatative result. TLC is far less sensitive than other tests. Low levels of substance abuse are not readily detected by TLC, so the meaning of screenings by TLC is confusing. Whether a sample is called positive or negative often depends on the concentration of the drug in the sample or the sensitivity cut-off of the test. The sensitivity cut-off of most TLC tests is between 1,000 and 2,000 nanograms per millileter (ng/ml). Some drugs are detectable only when they reach a concentration of more than 2,000 ng/ml, which makes them difficult to detect. Cut-off points for immunoassay tests, in contraast, are often 100 ng/ml and can be even lower. A negative TLC result may simply mean that the method is not sensitive enough to detect the drug in the sample. TLC also suffers from low specificity, as do immunoassay tests. TLC is used as a broad screen for drugs because it is fast, inexpensive, and does not require sophisticated instrumentation.

TLC is often used in medical settings to detect recent high-dose drug abuse and toxic levels of drugs. It is an ideal test for an emergency room, where the drugs taken are unknown and quick measurement of toxic levels is necessary.

Do-It-Yourself Drug Testing

As early as 1987, home-based drug tests began to appear on the market. One early kit called AWARE® was developed by American Drug Screens of Dallas. The kit, complete with specimen bottles and mailing tubes, was marketed toward parents who are concerned that their children may be using drugs. Samples were mailed to a processing lab, with results returned within two weeks.

Many labs offer testing on the Internet. If you worry that you might test positive you could test yourself through an independent service or with a home testing kit. Some people who hope to pass the test by switching or adulterating samples use independent testing to try out their strategies for beating the test in advance.

Sensitivity And Specificity

Test "sensitivity" is a measure of the smallest amount of the drug that can be detected in the urine sample. Specificity of a test is its ability to distinguish one drug from another. Sensitivity of the screening test should be set appropriately for the goals of the test.

Cut-Off Level

Cut-off level and detection limit are two factors influencing a test's sensitivity. "Cut-off level" is the value above which a specimen is considered positive and below which it is considered negative. Screening assays and confirmatory assays differ in their specificity and sensitivity so that screening (EIA) cut-off concentrations are different than the confirmatory cut-off concentrations.

Typically the first test given is for broad screening and is inexpensive. These include the EMIT®, TLC, or RIA, which are relatively sensitive, and can detect most drugs or metabolites in the system. They give an on-off, positive or negative result. If there is a positive, it should be confirmed by a different test. The most credible confirmation is GC/MS, which is considerably more expensive. The confirmation test used should be more specific in its results. There are volume discounts available on large numbers of similar tests from the same accounts. On the other hand, specially designed tests which have to conform to rigorous standards are very much more expensive.

Confirmation Of Positive Results

All urine samples reported positive should be analyzed a second time by a different testing method. Both tests should give a positive result before a positive report is made. This process is called "confirmation".

CHAPTER 5

Drug Testing Is Hazardous To Your Work

Most employers operate under the illusion that drug testing is objective and scientific. In fact, it is far from foolproof. Testing-caused problems can diminish your freedom and cost you your job. First of all, the results may not be valid! You might test positive when you haven't used drugs, for example. A positive test doesn't prove you were impaired at the time you were tested, but most employers think it does! Nonetheless, if you test positive, your employer could act upon that erroneous assumption so that you face certain humiliation and possible reprimand, even being fired. Drug testing is hazardous to your work!

Validity

Drug testing is not perfect. In a famous study, the Center for Disease Control (CDC) sent samples containing known quantities of barbiturates, amphetamines, methadone, cocaine, codeine, and morphine to 13 laboratories conducting tests for methadone treatment facilities. The labs didn't know they were being evaluated. The CDC reported error rates of up to 94 percent in false negatives (labs unable to detect drugs present in the samples) and up to 66 percent in false positive errors (detecting drugs actually not present in the samples). Those early testing labs operated at a much lower standard than today's labs because methodology and reliability have improved considerably since then. But problems continue.

Many Errors

Errors can be made anywhere in the process from collection, identification of the sample, to reporting of the results. "False positive" means that a drug-free sample is reported positive for drugs. "False negative" means that a sample containing drugs is reported as drug-free. False positives can be caused by sloppy lab work where technicians contaminate your sample, or by reading a different substance—a "cross-reactant"—as a drug.

Commenting on the CDC study, David Smith, Director of the Haight Ashbury Free Clinic said, "in many cases the labs would have done a better job if they had poured the urine down the drain and flipped a coin." On the other hand, Bob Fogerson, Quality Assurance Manager at PharmChem, argues that "it is not valid to conclude drug testing cannot be done accurately just because it has not been done accurately." Meanwhile, you—the employee—become the guinea pig used to develop testing that *can be* accurate!

Problems of laboratory performance, faulty confirmation, legal action, and carelessness began appearing almost immediately in mass-screenings of enlisted military personnel for drugs. The American Civil Liberties Union estimated that as many as 30,000—nearly 30 percent of Air Force and Army personnel—who tested positive might be eligible to have disciplinary charges against them dismissed due to errors. The Navy suffered similar problems. They found that 2,000 of 6,000 tests ordered analyzed could not be "scientifically substantiated as positive"—and an additional 2,000 test results were of questionable validity because documentation was missing.

False Positives For Opiates

One of the most difficult tasks for Medical Review Officers (MROs) and others interpreting urine drug screening results, is the opiate positive. Approximately 70% of DOT (Department of Transportation) opiates positives are due to poppy seeds. Prescription drugs and poppy seed consumption as well as use of over-the-counter medications give positive results for opiate use. Interpretation of urinary opiate results is fairly complex.

TOXNET LABORATORY reports that they have demonstrated that poppy seeds contained in bakery products such as bagels can result in positive opiate (morphine) results at low levels (below 3000 ng/ml). Codeine may also be found after poppy seed ingestion, but morphine is predominant. Although morphine is an ordinary metabolite of codeine, the presence of codeine in poppy seeds probably comes from the poppy seeds themselves rather than as a metabolite. Generally high levels of codeine, above the morphine level, probably indicate codeine ingestion.

After false positives disrupted thousands of DOT employees' lives, the government *finally* amended the Mandatory Guidelines for Federal Workplace Drug Testing Programs by increasing the cut-off (from 300 to 2000 ng/ml) and confirmatory levels for opiates, which took effect May 1998.

The Two Bagel Breakfast

A preplacement urine screened positive for opiates by radioimmunoassay and EMIT®. Gas chromatography/mass spectrometry (GC/MS) identified 487 ng/ml morphine. The individual denied opioid abuse. Inquiry by the examining medical center revealed a diet consisting of a Burger King hamburger the night before the specimen was taken and a breakfast, apparently usual, of two bagels from the university snack bar. The individual appeared to be quite normal. TOXNET LABORATORY obtained a bagel from the snack bar. Pulverization of a few poppy seeds used as decoration on the bagel resulted in positive immunoassay (RIA and EMIT®) responses. A TOXNET LABORATORY toxicologist volunteered to eat the bagel and collect urine post-dose. The first urine, three hours post dose, resulted in an opiate level, as determined by Roche radioimmunoassay (RIA), of 250 ng/ml. By six hours post-dose the level had dropped to about 60 ng/ml and was negative (sensitivity 30 ng/ml) by 12 hours post dose.

TOXNET LABORATORY obtained a bottle of Schillings poppy seeds, imported from the Netherlands, from a local market and had the laboratory volunteer eat three teaspoons, six grams, of the seeds. The first urine was collected six hours post-dose and had the highest opiate level, approximately 1200 ng/ml as determined by the Roche radioimmunoassay (RIA). Levels twelve hours post-dose dropped to about 250 ng/ml, and the urine was negative by twenty-four hours post-dose (sensitivity 30 ng/ml).

TOXNET LABORATORY
LabWorld@Healthy.net

Hemp Seed Foods

TOXNET Laboratory showed that cookies made from cannabis sativa seed—otherwise known as hemp seed can cause a positive urine test for cannabis. Although wild strains of hemp cannabis are very low in THC, they still contain enough to create a urinary drug positive after ingesting the seeds. Like poppy seeds, the genetic origin of the seeds determines how much drug they contain. Hemp raised for fiber contain much less THC than modern strains selectively bred for the psychoactive THC content.

TOXNET analyzed urine of people who ate hemp cookies from the Hungry Bear Hemp Foods company called "Seedy Sweeties with Nuts" and "Seedy Sweeties with Sunflower Seeds." Three volunteers at TOXNET collected preingestion urines as a zero baseline, ate one or two of the 42.5 gram bars, and collected urines post-dose.

All three volunteers screened above 50 ng/ml and confirmed positive above 15 ng/ml for THC after eating the hemp seed bars. Oral ingestion of these bars produced urinary positives within four hours and one lasted as long as 48 hours above the cut-offs. Peak urinary excretion occurred about 8 hours after ingestion.

Human Error

Most errors are related to poor management, inadequate personnel, broken chain of custody, faulty maintenance of equipment, and faulty transmissions of reports and records, rather than to the tests themselves. Sometimes the problem is contamination of glassware with drug-positive samples, which causes an estimated false positive rate of 3 to 5 percent.

Manufacturers of drug tests claim their instruments are 95 to 99 percent accurate at detecting traces of drugs in urine, when their own lab employees operate the machines while closely watched for proficiency. Manufacturers claim that the gas chromatography/mass spectrometry is nearly 100 percent accurate. But these high accuracy rates hold only when the lab operators are extremely proficient and diligent. Such ideal conditions hardly ever exist in practice. Commercial drug test manufacturers sell and lease their instruments to private labs and hospitals. The College of American Pathologists (CAP), the American Association of Bioanalysts (AAB) and the American Association of Clinical Chemistry (AAC) have programs monitoring the quality of work done at these labs.

The reality is that the machines are only as reliable as the people operating them. Careless, overworked, or incompetent operators can misuse the machines in innumerable ways, yielding false positive results on clean urine specimens and other errors.

Regulation Needed

At a California State Senate Hearing to evaluate the need for lab regulations, Dr. David Smith of the Haight-Ashbury Free Clinic was adamant in pointing out that "in a random or mass testing, without probable cause, error is inevitable." Typically, the cheapest tests—which give only a positive or a negative result and are subject to some error—are used. Unqualified clerks are often delegated the responsibility of obtaining samples. Consequently, errors in mass testing are quite possible. Smith pointed out that many employers are not adequately informed. Often the lab technicians themselves do not understand the testing process or how data is to be interpreted.

Causes Of Errors in Testing

- *Improper laboratory procedures*
- *Inadvertent switching of samples*
- *Paperwork being lost or damaged*
- *Passive inhalation*
- *Cross-reactivity with other, legal drugs*
- *Tampering with samples*
- *Unknown reasons*

False Positives

False positive refers to a positive result on a drug-free sample. False positives may occur due to testing methodology or because equipment was contaminated. In drug testing it is common, especially in private companies, to have non-specialist personnel carrying out on-site specimen collection.

A high false-positive rate isn't that critical in research, drug abuse treatment programs, and other nonpunitive situations. On the other hand, in drug testing directed at probationers, pre-employment, promotion candidates, or job-fitness evaluations, reporting a positive urine test takes on great personal and social significance. Potential repercussions of a positive drug test result in an employment context can be catastrophic.

Positives in "initial" or "screening" tests should be confirmed by using a test that is based on *a different chemical methodology*. That is, a chromatography test should be used to confirm immunoassay test results, because they utilize different methods, whereas *EMIT® and RIA should never be used to confirm other immunoassays.* Using TLC to confirm an RIA result is valid because it is of the chromatography group. There are other considerations in using TLC, however. The TLC is ordinarily a first step or screening test, and subject to more error than the GC or GC/MS. If confirmation of a positive can have a significant impact on you, then you'll want most accurate test available to be used. This would call for the GC/MS, and sometimes a drug test on a blood sample would be indicated, especially in post-accident testing to determine impairment by drug use. Unfortunately, not all employers follow this basic rule.

Cross-Reactivity

Cross-reactivity was studied by Allen and Stiles, who tested 161 prescription and over-the-counter drugs with the EMIT®-d.a.u. screens for opiates, amphetamines, barbiturates, benzodiazepines, methadone, propoxyphene, and cocaine metabolite. They found that 65 of the prescription drugs and over-the-counter products showed some cross-reactivity, including values above cut-off. Fortunately, most of the positives required concentrations that are not achievable in human urine and do not present practical problems. Presumably that should give a little comfort. But the fact remains if you use a prescription or over-the-counter medicine before a drug test you could test positive.

Appedrine® diet pills tested positive for amphetamines. Ibuprofen, the anti-inflammatory agent in Advil® and Nuprin®, can produce false positives when testing for marijuana. About 150 legal over-the-counter medications, especially those containing synthetic compounds like phenylpropanolamine, have been reported as causing positives in amphetamine tests, and can also cause a false positive in a methedrine test. Some sources claim that the cocaine EMIT® test can yield a positive if the person being tested drank large quantities of tea. Antihistamines may cause a false positive for PCP.

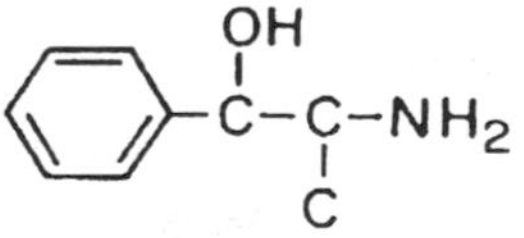

Phenylpropanolamine

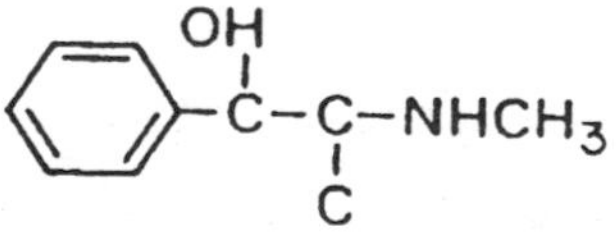

Ephedrine

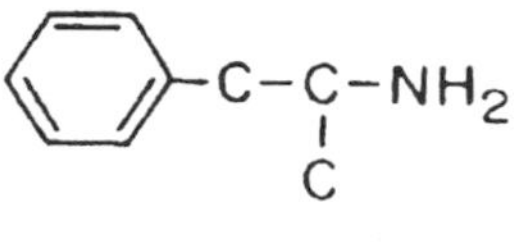

Amphetamine

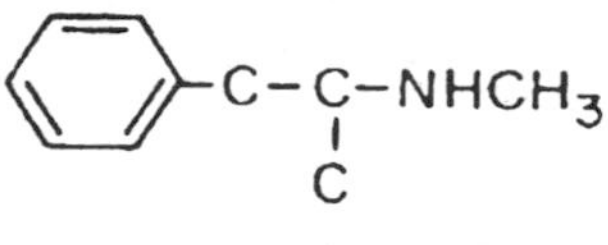

Methamphetamine

The molecular diagram showing the similarity between phenylpropanolamine and ephedrine which are found in many over-the-counter medicines and amphetamine and methamphetamine. These similarities are the reason that many over-the-counter medicines cause cross-reactivity and false positives. (From John P. Morgan, M.D., "Problems of Mass Urine Screening of Misused Drugs," pg. 26 *Substance Abuse in the Workplace.*)

Syva and Roche, which manufacture the EMIT® and Abuscreen® tests, say they inform labs that the tests are "class assays," designed to detect broad categories for drug-like substances in the urine. This is particularly true for amphetamines and opiates. For example, the heroin screen looks for substances *similar* in basic structure to morphine, the basic opiate molecule. Opioid substances include dextromethorphan, a nonintoxicating cough suppressant found in common, uncontrolled, drugstore nostrums like Nyquil®, Doco Children's Cough Syrup®, Comtrex®, Peda-care® and Benylin®. EMIT® and Abuscreen® both yield amphetamine positives on phenylpropanolamine or PPA, a mild decongestant which is an active ingredient in dozens of drugstore medications, including Alka-Selzer Plus®, as well as popular weight-reduction preparations like Dexatrim® and Dietac®.

Cross-Reactivity With EMIT® At ≥100 MCG/ML

Generic name	Brand name	Cross-reactivity
Amitriptyline HCI	Elavil®	Methadone
Carisoprodol	Soma®	Methadone
Clindinium bromide	Quarzan®	Benzodiazepine
Cloxacillin Na	Tegopen®	Benzodiazepine
Diphenhydramine HCI	Benadry®	Methadone
Imipramine HCI	Tofranil®	Methadone
Isoxuprine HCI	Vasodilan®	Amphetamine
Orphenadrine citrate	Norflex®	Methadone
Perphenazine	Trilafon®	Benzodiazepine
Promethazine HCI	Phenergan®	Methadone & Opiate
Thiethylperzine maleate	Torecan®	Methadone
Tripelennamine HCI	Pyribenzamine®	Benzodiazepine & Methadone

Values are equal to or greater than 100 micrograms per milliliter.
Source: Allen & Stiles.

Syva reported that ephedrine cross-reacts with amphetamines on both the EMIT® and the Abuscreen®. Ephedrine is a decongestant in common over-the-counter medicines.

The table shows over-the-counter medicines that often cause cross-reactivity on EMIT® tests, which is serious because the medicines are widely used for common ailments. If you've taken an over-the-counter pain or a menstrual cramp preparation you could test positive and find yourself having to prove you're not a drug abuser. If you have arthritis or a sports injury and take a prescription anti-inflamatory, like Naproxyn, you could test positive for steroids. You could test like a speed-freak if you have a cold and used a nasal decongestant, because most contain ephedrine or phenypropanolamine, which cause a positive for amphetamines. You could test positive for opiates if you've used Vicks Formula 44M® or eaten a poppy seed bagal. You could test positive for cocaine if you're taking the antibiotic amoxicillin. Pretty scary!

You can be honestly drug free and still test positive on a drug screening test—and so could the guy at the next desk. If this happens to you, you will be suspected of abusing drugs. Cross-reactivity is a problem that has not been solved and continues to be misunderstood by many companies. As you can see, even if you have used no drugs, not even any drug store medicines, you can still test positive because of testing errors, screw-ups at the lab, or cross-reactivity. Being tested for drugs is hazardous to your job because if you test positive you could lose it. There could be problems with your test and you could come up positive.

Be smart. Get informed. Be proactive. Prepare to pass the test!

CHAPTER 6

You Have A Right To Privacy

You've heard the retort, "Well, if have nothing to hide you shouldn't mind being tested for drugs." On the contrary, you do have something to guard against: invasion of your privacy. The "right to privacy" is, in the words of the eminent Supreme Court Justice Louis Brandeis, "the most comprehensive of rights and the most valued by civilized men."

Workplace drug testing is an invasion of your privacy because it can disclose details about your private life far beyond drug use, such as if you are pregnant, consume alcohol, are being treated for various medical conditions or are taking Prozac™, for example. You probably don't want your company knowing these things about you—they are private and not the business of your boss.

Reasonable Expectation Of Privacy

Privacy is one of your fundamental rights. Stated in legal terms, you have a "reasonable expectation" of privacy when using a toilet or urinal in your workplace. You don't expect to be watched while you pee and being observed by an agent of your employer is a violation of your reasonable expectation of privacy. If you can demonstrate that your expectation of privacy has been violated, you may have grounds for legal action.

Your expectation of privacy can be reduced if your company has clearly informed you (along with your co-workers) about the drug testing program, when and how it will occur, and so forth. This notification reduces, but does not eliminate, expectation of privacy. Information about the company's drug testing program is usually included in the employee manual and in documents you receive when applying for the job.

But there's a loophole in our privacy rights and that is when your employer has a "compelling" interest, in which case your "expectation of privacy" is diminished. It is because of this loophole that your company can invade your privacy and "search" your bodily fluids. We'll explore each of these aspects in the next several chapters discussing your rights and the interest of the public. First, an exploration of your right to privacy.

Gathering Confidential Information

Drug testing involves gathering very personal information about you. You are required to disclose medicines, over-the-counter preparations and illicit drugs you have taken, for example. And information is gathered from the test itself. Fortunately, your company is not permitted to gather any and all information on you as it pleases. There are restrictions—which are constantly being eroded. The company has to have a particular purpose to gather private information on you—especially when it comes to "medical" information.

Don't ever give over your medical records or sign authorizations for your company to obtain your records without first finding out exactly what their purpose is in reviewing them. And if you do give your company permission to peruse your medical records, make sure that they promise—in writing—to maintain strict confidentiality.

Access to and release of medical information is highly regulated and most states protect the right to privacy of medical records. The degree of privacy afforded under State Constitutions varies widely from state to state. Information containing medical, psychiatric, or psychological material is classified as "confidential information." It simply cannot be obtained without your prior written voluntary consent. (You can get information about your state's protections, or lack thereof, in regards to drug testing from *Guide To State And Federal Drug-Testing Laws,* complied by the Institute For A Drug-Free Workplace in Washington D.C., www.drugfreeworkplace.org)

If you test positive your company is required to maintain the privacy of that data. They cannot give data to your supervisor or co-workers or anyone else. If results from your drug test, including suspicions arising from the test, are shared with third parties, including other employees who have no need to know, you could have a claim for defamation of character—particularly if the findings turn out to be incorrect. There may also be grounds for defamation lawsuits if your employer tells a third party the reason for any adverse action against you, such as termination, especially if the third party is a prospective employer.

Who Has A Right To Privacy?

Federal and State Constitutions protect all citizens against unreasonable *government* searches and seizures of person and property. Federal protection applies to actions by government officials, not behavior of private individuals, organizations or businesses. Constitutional protections don't apply to privately held companies. On the other hand, if a private employer uses the police or other government officials in the course of invading your privacy, then you might claim the employer is acting as an "agent" of the State, in which case Constitutional standards are usually applied.

In general, if you work for a private company you must look to your State's laws to protect your right to privacy. For the most part, as an employee of private company you have little protection against the Mandatory Drug Testing Programs adopted by many companies, including several in the Fortune 500. The ACLU believes that it is unfair that government workers are protected in their rights to privacy, but their counterparts in private industry are not.

State Privacy Protection

Ten States—Alaska, California, Florida, Hawaii, Illinois, Louisiana, Montana, New York, South Carolina, and Washington—have express privacy provisions in their Constitutions. Some State Constitutions have a more developed right to privacy than the Federal Constitution. For example, the California Constitution under Article 1, Section 1, specifically guarantees a person's right to privacy, and this provision has been interpreted to apply to *both* private and governmental activities.

California's Right To Privacy

All people are by nature free and independent, and have certain inalienable rights. Among these are enjoying and defending life and liberty, acquiring, possessing, and protecting property, and pursuing and obtaining safety, happiness, and privacy.

Constitution of the State of California
Article 1, Section 1

A leading California case addressing the general privacy rights is *White* v. *David.* The California Supreme Court ruled that the California right to privacy prevents the government and businesses from secretly gathering personal information, from overly broad collection and retention of unnecessary personal information, and from improper use or disclosure of properly gathered personal information. The Court set forth a list of "mischiefs" the right of privacy was meant to correct.

White Mischiefs

1. *Government snooping and the secret gathering of personal information.*
2. *The overly broad collection and retention of unnecessary personal information by government and business interests*
3. *The improper use of information properly obtained for a specific purpose, for example, use for another purpose, or the disclosure of it to a third party.*
4. *The lack of a reasonable check on the accuracy of existing records.*

The White decision addressed secret or overly broad information gathering and improper disclosure. The White "mischiefs" may not apply to employee drug testing, however.

In the first ruling of its kind in California, a State Appeals Court in 1989 upheld a private company's drug testing of its job applicants, regardless of the safety-sensitive nature of the position. The 3-to-0 decision upheld a pre-employment drug and alcohol screening program at Matthew Bender & Co., a subsidiary of the Times Mirror Co. The Court specified that its ruling applied only to testing of applicants and not to employees, whose privacy rights against testing may be greater.

Compelling Interests

The right to privacy is not absolute, however, it must be offset against other compelling interests. In the use of drugs, for example, at least one California Court has held that an individual has no Constitutional privacy right to use or possess cocaine at home (*People* v. *Davis*). The decision in *NORML* v. *Gain* established that California does not recognize a Constitutional right to use or possess marijuana in one's own home. How the passage of voter initiatives allowing medical marijuana in California and other states will impact will undoubtedly play itself out in Court.

An infringement of a Constitutional privacy right must be justified by a "compelling interest". Showing that the State's interest cannot be satisfied in a less intrusive manner is generally necessary. Justification for the privacy intrusion must be substantial to meet the compelling interest test·

The right to pursue and obtain safety, to preserve and protect property, and to pursue and obtain privacy are all protected by the Constitution. Drug testing court cases in California often pit the Constitutional interests of employers, employees, co-workers and the public against one another.

How to resolve the clash of the Constitution rights of safety and privacy is an unresolved California Constitutional question. The use by police of drunk driver "checkpoints" that involve stopping and checking drivers at random, without any individual suspicion, was approved by the California Supreme Court (*Ingersoll* v. *Palmer*) and may help set the standard for the future of drug testing. The Court found that right to privacy was safeguarded by prior general public notice of location of the checkpoints and by stopping each motorist only very briefly if there is not suspicion of wrongdoing.

However, as civil rights attorneys Edward Chen and John True point out, "no one has ever suggested that motorists be subject to random detentions and urine tests wherein they run the risk of losing their driver's license if such urine tests come up positive.... even sobriety checkpoints require probable cause based upon observation of behavior and appearance together with failed performance of a field sobriety test before the police can require the production of blood or urine."

Privacy Off The Job

You probably have an expectation that what you do in your off-duty time, away from the job, is your business and not the business of your employer. Generally, the Courts would support that opinion. There are exceptions, however. For example, if the company can show a relationship between off-duty behavior and the job, disciplinary actions may be taken. Even for illegal behavior, such as the use of illicit drugs, it is still the employer's burden to establish the link between that misconduct and your job performance. For example, what link can be shown between occasional weekend use of marijuana and the job of a stock boy, clerk, or even a professional? It could be argued that casual use in this situation is no more damaging or job-related than casual use of alcohol. The burden is on the employer to prove this link. Of course, some employers ignore this and run over your rights.

There are several standards generally used to evaluate off-duty misconduct and whether or not it constitutes grounds for "discipline". These standards include injury to the company, inability or unsuitability to perform, threatening the safety of the public and co-workers, and damaging interactions with other employers.

The idea that drug or alcohol testing may infringe on non-work activities merits consideration. Drug tests can identify drug use during your off-duty hours. An employer's interest in your personal matters is not compelling unless your use of drugs affects the workplace. The way that companies get around this little sticky point is to issue official "policies" prohibiting you from having any drugs in your system while on the job. Some employers, who feel that your use of drugs while off-duty is itself a hazard that they have a responsibility to curb, have company policies that require you be drug-free at all times. A positive drug test shows that there were traces of drugs in your system during working hours, which violates the company's anti-drug rules—even though you were not impaired when tested.

> *May employers exercise control over off-the-job conduct simply because there is some correlation with job performance? If so, employers would have the right to control many aspects of worker personal life which could influence performance and productivity, including domestic disputes, personal financial woes, sleeping and eating habits, cigarette smoking and indeed any personal condition which affects an employee's overall physical and mental health. This argument has no logical limit, and it leads logically to frightening consequences. If drug tests are permitted, why not psychological tests and genetic screenings?*
>
> Edward Chen & John True
> Civil Liberties Attorneys

Privacy Is Evolving

Differences exist between Federal and State laws. For example, consider the Oregon election of November 1986. At the peak of the national "War on Drugs," Oregonians could have legalized marijuana use in their State, even while in the rest of the Nation's employees in private and public business were being tested, put into treatment programs, and sometimes fired for the use of marijuana. The Oregon ballot contained an initiative signed by 90,000 Oregonians to legalize marijuana. While the initiative was defeated by a 2 to 1 vote, it was on the ballot nonetheless.

In the Oregn initiative, "private" means "not public." In common-sense terms, private means that marijuana could not be used in a location where it would intrude upon the sensibilities of other people who might be offended. This notion of private is comparable to the definition used in the statutes prohibiting public indecency or public drunkenness. Had the initiative passed, it still would have been illegal to possess marijuana in parks, school grounds, or any place visible to the public.

During the Oregon initiative process, Governor Vic Atiyeh rejected a proposal by the President's Commission on Organized Crime to test all State workers for drug use. Atiyeh was quoted as saying he would not require drug testing as a condition of employment in the State of Oregon, because in his opinion it was "not necessary," and that drug use by State workers in Oregon was not a "major problem." As far as Governor Atiyeh was concerned, what employees did in their off-duty time was none of his business as long as it did not negatively affect their job performance. The Governor further cautioned private employers against using drug testing on employees, because in his opinion, such drug testing "involves an unfair presumption of guilt."

Another dramatic instance of the different interpretation of privacy in a State versus Federal context is provided by the Alaska Supreme Court's unanimous ruling on marijuana in *Ravin* v. *State.* The Court ruled that the Alaskan Constitution protects an individual's privacy, and agreed with the NORML and ACLU attorneys that marijuana did not represent a significant enough risk to society to allow the State to invade an individual's privacy. In the years following the Court's decision, several surveys indicate basic support for the reform. If anything, the surveys demonstrate support for legalizing the sales of small amounts of marijuana and perhaps total legalization.

The Supreme Court of Alaska discussed the Ravin decision in *Harrison* v. *State.* A State trooper had been arrested in a dry county—a county where alcohol is illegal—with alcohol in his possession. The trooper claimed that the Ravin case provided a precedent for his possession of alcohol. He argued that if you are allowed to possess marijuana, you are surely allowed to possess alcohol. The Alaskan Supreme Court saw things differently, however. They examined the effects that alcohol was having in Alaskan society and compared that to marijuana. They found that there was no comparison, and that the State had more cause to regulate, even prohibit, alcohol than it did marijuana.

CHAPTER 7

It's A Search

Americans have a long tradition of opposing general searches of innocent people which began in Colonial America, when King George's forces searched people indiscriminately in order to uncover a few who were committing offenses against the crown. These general searches were deeply resented. After the Revolution, the experience of the unfairness of the indiscriminate searches fresh in the new American psyche, the Fourth Amendment was passed. It states that authorities cannot search everyone, innocent and guilty alike, to find the few who are guilty. There must be reasonable suspicion of a particular person before subjecting him or her to intrusive or degrading searches.

Arguments surrounding the right to privacy hinge on the interpretation and application of several key terms and ideas. These include "search," "seizure," "reasonableness" (as in "reasonable expectation of privacy" and "reasonable suspicion"), "probable cause," "compelling interest" (as in "a compelling interest to protect public safety" and "voluntary consent") and "particularized suspicion".

The fundamental legal question is whether drug testing in the workplace is compatible with the protection of personal privacy embodied in the Fourth Amendment's prohibition of unreasonable searches and seizures. Indiscriminate drug testing threatens traditional Fourth Amendment values. Perhaps more than any other provision of the Bill of Rights, the Fourth Amendment expresses an essential quality of democracy—the defense of personal dignity against violation by the State. We ought not experiment with these rights. They are fragile. Once damaged they are not easily repaired. Once lost they are not easily recovered.

Adherence to tested Fourth Amendment principles is particularly important when, as now, there is widespread clamor for a simple solution to a serious social problem. The saddest episodes in American Constitutional history have been those occasions, such as the internment of Americans of Japanese descent during World War II, when we have bent our principles to the zealotry of the moment. What is expedient is not necessarily fair, or Constitutional. A war on drugs is a good idea, but not if its first casualty is the Bill of Rights.

Office of the Attorney General
Maryland

Is Urine Testing A Search?

A preliminary question is whether the collection and testing of a urine specimen is a "search" and "seizure" within the meaning of the Fourth Amendment. A *search* occurs when an expectation of privacy that society is prepared to consider reasonable is infringed. A *seizure* of property occurs when there is some meaningful interference with an individual's possessory interests in that property.

The Supreme Court ruled in *National Treasury Employees Union* v. *United States Customs Service* that taking a urine specimen for drug testing purposes *is*, in fact, a search under the Fourth Amendment. However, it is not necessarily a violation of the Amendment, because only unreasonable searches and seizures are prohibited. So an inquiry into the reasonableness is essential. The greater or more demeaning the intrusion, the more substantial the reason for conducting the search must be. The right to "be free from unreasonable governmental intrusion" applies whenever an individual may harbor a *reasonable expectation of privacy.* An expectation of privacy is legitimate in Fourth Amendment terms if the person has an actual or subjective expectation of privacy, and the expectation is one that society is prepared to recognize as reasonable. The Maryland Attorney General concluded, "in our view, State employees as a group have an actual, subjective expectation that their bodily functions will not be subject to government intrusion. Nothing about State employment gives employees reason to suppose that their urination is subject to supervisory inspection and probing. It states the obvious to say that State employees, like everybody else, expect to dispose of their wastes in private."

Search And Seizure

A drug test is, in fact, a search and seizure. In order to conduct such a search of your urine, especially when there is the possibility of adverse action, such a seizure of your job — your livelihood—that search must be reasonable. In most cases, before your employer can test you for drugs, the testing program should have been announced well in advance as company policy and described in detail in writing to you. Drug testing should not be just popped on you. If it is, then it is considered less "reasonable" because you have to "consent" before proceeding with an intrusive search. Getting the sample to test should always be conducted so that your dignity is preserved. You should never be subjected to humiliation in the course of giving a sample. Without a properly announced "search policy", it is questionable if your employer is legally allowed to search your purse, briefcase, backpack or a lunch box stored in a locker. Searches are a very legally sensitive issue and if you are subjected to a search on the job, you should respectfully but firmly state your objection. Whether or not you should stick to your guns and refuse the search is a serious question you will need to weigh. You will be suspected of holding contraband—at the very least. Whatever you decide, maintain your composure—don't give any behavioral evidence for them to point to—and document everything that happens in writing.

These days most employers are smart enough to exercise caution in taking possession of personal property. They call in the police to take possession of the evidence instead. If you get entangled in this unfortunate circumstance and your employer takes any evidence before the police get there, any grounds for criminal prosecution might be affected by mishandling of the evidence.

Search Must Be Reasonable

An employer's testing policy is likely to be upheld when there is a strong indication that you had recently used or were under the influence of drugs or alcohol. In general, the rules for violation of privacy have to do with "reasonable suspicion" and "probable cause."

Factors Affecting Reasonableness Of Drug Tests

- *Accurate test methodology*
- *Reliable chain of custody*
- *Safety, security or integrity of company business goals*
- *Documentation of past drug use in company*

- *Inappropriateness of ineffectiveness of other, less intrusive means of achieving the company's goals.*
- *Efforts to minimize intrusiveness of specimen collection.*
- *Procedures for protection of confidential records and test data.*
- *Availability of rehabilitation option or periodic monitoring before discipline results.*
- *Existence of clear notice of the program and its requirements that may result in discipline or termination.*
- *Existence of other safeguards against error, such as permitting employees to explain positive results that might be in error and retesting the same sample in questioned cases.*
- *For random testing there should be additional justification on the basis of substantial safety or security factors; difficulty in monitoring employee performance for signs of drug use.*

From William Adams, The Dos, Don'ts and Whys of Drug Testing, *Labor and Employment Law Update*, Orrick, Herrington & Sutcliffe.

Determining Reasonableness

Reasonableness depends on two factors: *the degree of intrusiveness* of the search and seizure; and *the public interests at stake.* A search in the service of public safety in the case of an airplane pilot is considered more reasonable than a random search of your locker, for example.

Testing that does not involve observation of you giving the sample is less intrusive and therefore considered more reasonable. However, such testing is considered less effective. The more effective type of testing would be actual close observation you peeing to prevent tampering with the sample. But this is also more intrusive and thus less reasonable, unless there is a very strong reason to actually suspect you of using drugs.

Reasonable Suspicion Standards

Reasonable suspicion may be based on indications that you are under the influence of drugs, including slurred speech, accidents, frequent absences, tardiness, and early departures from work. Since reasonable suspicion is established by combining facts with judgment, it is not possible to predict or describe every situation which may create a reasonable suspicion.

Reduced Expectation Of Privacy

The context of the situation is very important in establishing the reasonableness or unreasonableness of a search. In part, context entails the particular requirements of performing a given job and whether you could or could not threaten public safety.

Some categories of State employees can reasonably be expected to have somewhat diminished expectations of privacy, given the nature of their work. Someone who becomes a police officer or firefighter must know what the job entails and the special obligation of those who enforce the law to obey it themselves. Hence police officers may, in certain circumstances, enjoy less Constitutional protection than the ordinary citizen. But even where police officers and firefighters have diminished protection, they may be tested only if the reasonable suspicion standard is met. For example, in the *McDonnell* v. *Hunter* case, in which prison guards' cars were being searched, testing was approved only on the basis of reasonable suspicions based on specific observable facts and reasonable inferences drawn from these facts in light of experience that a given employee was abusing drugs.

In the case of *Capua* v. *Plainfield,* an investigation began when officials in Plainfield, N.J., received an anonymous tip that some of the city's police and firefighters were using illicit drugs. The city cracked down, staging a surprise urine test for all 244 members of the police and fire departments. Twenty employees, including two cops, tested positive for marijuana or cocaine and were given the option of resigning or being suspended. Sixteen suspended firefighters filed suit in Federal court, and U.S. District Court Judge H. Lee Sarokin ruled that Plainfield's "mass round-up urinalysis" violated the Constitutional prohibition against unreasonable search and seizure. "The threat posed by widespread use is real. The need to combat it is manifest," Judge Sarokin wrote in his decision, "But it is important not to permit fear and panic to overcome our fundamental principles and protections."

However, in the Plainfield case, the Court also held that testing of these employees under the "individualized reasonable suspicion" standard would meet Fourth Amendment standards. In other words, the mistake that the city of Plainfield made was conducting a wholesale mass testing unannounced, without any reasonable suspicion of particular individuals.

In *Amalgamated Transit Employee* v. *Suscy,* a Transit Authority employee came under suspicion by two supervisors who believed that he was under the influence and therefore had him tested. In the ensuing lawsuit, the Court held that the blood and urine testing of this municipal bus driver was permissible under the Fourth Amendment, citing the valid interest in protecting the public. This decision reinforced the notion that an employer should be able to test employees if public safety is an overriding concern.

In *National Treasury Employees Union* v. *United States Customs Service* and *Skinner* v. *Railway Labor Executives Associations,* both plaintiffs argued that "particularized suspicion" was essential to justify compulsory drug testing of employees. But the Supreme Court disagreed and found that drug testing can be Constitutional even without particularized suspicion that an individual employee is, in fact, a drug user.

Supreme Court Justice Anthony Kennedy, writing for the majority in the 1989 landmark *Skinner* v. *Railway Labor Executives Associations* decision, agreed that drug tests are "searches" according to the Fourth Amendment. But he concluded that the search was reasonable when the "diminished" privacy interests of railway workers were balanced against the "compelling" interest in deterring drug use on the rails. "The expectations of privacy of covered employees are diminished by reason of their participation in an industry that is regulated pervasively to insure safety," said Justice Kennedy. In the related decision of *National Treasury Employees Union* v. *United States Custom Service,* he concluded that Customs employees who carry firearms and those involved in drug interdiction have the same "diminished expectation of privacy."

Giving Sample In Private

Some people have suggested that drug testing will be less intrusive if your actual giving of the sample is not observed, since most people do not expect to be observed while they are urinating. However, the absence of supervision means that you could substitute someone else's "clean" urine or otherwise tamper with the sample.

There are methods other than observation to ensure your specimen's integrity. The Federal Testing Program calls for supervision of your urination if "the agency has reason to believe that [you] may alter or substitute the specimen to be provided". For Fourth Amendment purposes, a less intrusive but also less effective program is as problematic as a more intrusive but more effective one.

> *If a blanket search program has little or no effectiveness, it is in substance merely a kind of harassment, a show of power, or a 'fishing expedition,' and therefore, per se, unreasonable under the Fourth Amendment.*
>
> U.S. v. Davis

For Cause

An employer can increase reasonableness of drug testing by making sure it is done "for cause" which means that testing may occur when reasonable suspicion exists that you are using drugs—when there are specific objective facts and reasonable inferences in light of work experience that suggest you are using drugs. Staff members trained in recognizing signs of drug or alcohol abuse are able to make this kind of decision more reliably than untrained staff members, and their judgment will be more likely to withstand the scrutiny of a Court arbitrator.

It is impossible to fully define either "probable cause" or "reasonable suspicion" in the abstract. Reasonable suspicion is less stringent than probable cause. Even reasonable suspicion must be founded upon objective facts and rational inferences derived from practical experience, rather than unspecified suspicions, and must be directed toward a *particular person* to be tested.

Under a "for cause policy," a urine sample may be requested if a reasonable suspicion exists that you may be using drugs. Reasonable suspicion exists when there are specific objective facts and reasonable inferences from work experience that suggest you are under the influence of drugs. These may include slurred speech, an on-the-job accident, frequent absences, tardiness, or early departure from work. Since reasonable suspicion is established by combining fact and judgment, it is not possible to predict or describe every situation that may arouse reasonable suspicion.

There have been some significant Court cases around the issue of probable cause. For example, in *McDonnell* v. *Hunter*, the 8th Circuit Court declared unconstitutional routine searches of prison guards and their vehicles by the Iowa Department of Corrections on Fourth Amendment grounds. In this incident, the Court directed the department to revise search procedures so that they would be based only on probable cause.

Compelling Interest

The reasonableness of a search, including drug testing, is determined by balancing your privacy expectations against the government's interest in searching your bodily fluids. In *National Treasury Employees Union* v. *United States Customs Service*, the Supreme Court identified three governmental interests:

1) *"ensuring that front line drug interdiction personnel are physically fit, and have unimpeachable integrity and judgment;"*

2) *providing "effective measures to prevent the promotion of drug users to positions that require the incumbent to carry a firearm;" and*

3) *"protecting truly sensitive information from those who, under compulsion of circumstances or for other reasons, might compromise information."*

The Court weighed the interference with privacy resulting from giving urine for testing against the government's compelling interests. The Court concluded that, while requiring urine samples could interfere with privacy, the government's need to conduct such searches of employees engaged directly in drug interdiction and of those who carried firearms took precedence.

In another case involving drug testing, *Skinner* v. *Railway Labor Executives Associations,* the Court characterized the government's interest in promoting railroad safety through drug testing as "compelling" and, therefore, "not an undue infringement on the justifiable expectations of privacy of covered employees." While somewhat ambiguous, the Supreme Court's decision in the Customs case strongly suggests that protection of "sensitive information" related to drug enforcement investigation and national security are also compelling government interests. There is speculation that the decision may be applied to the broader context of commercially sensitive information. If future cases result in such rulings, then the range of employees subjected to testing could be greatly expanded—to employees with access to certain computer chips, for example.

Federal Constitutional Protections

In general, the Federal protection applies only when the challenged action is taken by government officials, not behavior of private individuals, organizations or businesses. In practice, however, private employers often use the State action requirement as a defense against Constitutional challenges to their drug testing policy. On the other hand, if a private employer uses the police or other government officials in the search, and the counter-claim is that the employer is acting as an "agent" of the State, then the Constitutional standard is usually applied.

CHAPTER 8

You Have A Right To Fair Treatment

Drug testing programs can violate your civil rights under the terms of the Fifth Amendment rights to be safe from self-incrimination and guarantee of due process.

The Fifth Amendment

No persons shall be held to answer for a capital, or otherwise infamous crime, unless on a presentment or indictment of a Grand Jury, except in cases rising in the land or naval forces, or in the Militia, when in actual service in time of war or public danger; nor shall any person be subject for the same offense to be twice put in jeopardy of life or limb; nor shall be compelled in any criminal case to be a witness against himself, nor be deprived of life, liberty, or property, without due process of law, nor shall private property be taken for use, without just compensation.

Self-incrimination defenses are not likely to stand, however. Blood and breath tests have been held not to violate your Fifth Amendment protections against self-incrimination. Urine testing is viewed as belonging in the same category as blood and breath tests. In fact, The Supreme Court, in *Skinner* v. *Railway Labor Executives Association* rejected the defense that urine drug testing is a form of self-incrimination.

Due Process

If you are *forced* to take a drug test and the process or results are *arbitrary*, it may be in violation of your rights under the Fifth Amendment. The question of fairness versus being arbitrary is usually answered by pointing to the accuracy of urine testing procedures and a factual demonstration that the procedure was followed.

A very dramatic case of drug testing abuse involved the Georgia Power Company. Leslie Price and Susan Register were two workers employed in a nuclear power plant. Register, a mechanical expediter, and Price, a quality-control inspector, were concerned about plant safety and reported apparent violations to the Nuclear Regulatory Commission. Subsequently, the two were told they had been "hot lined," and were ordered in for drug tests. Susan Register testified to being forced by a nurse to drop her pants to her ankles, bend over at the waist with her knees slightly bent, hold her right arm in the air, and with her left hand angle a specimen bottle between her legs. She described sobbing, wetting herself, and vomiting. She was fired for insubordination for refusing to take the test. Price gave her urine sample and was told that her sample was positive for marijuana. She was fired for misconduct. Had she been fired for drug use, the Nuclear Regulatory Commission might have ordered the company to recheck, at great cost, all the work she had inspected as a quality-controller. This is a dramatic example of how drug testing might be used to punish whistle-blowers.

Employers are not the only sources of potential abuse. A spiteful co-worker, for example, could report having "heard" rumors that you have been using drugs, causing you to be tested. Since these tests have a high rate of errors, you could come up with a positive test, even though you haven't used drugs. Some people are concerned that drug testing could be used in subtle ways to dissuade union organizing, or that particularly outspoken employees could be subjected to testing and have the future of their employment put in jeopardy.

Workers at Pacific Refining Company in Hercules, California, filed a class-action suit after the company ordered its employees to take urine tests. Hercules required all employees to come in, partly disrobe, and expose themselves so that a witness could verify the urine specimen. Three people refused to take the test and were fired, even though the company said that employees who tested positive would not be fired. The company said it had to fire those who refused because they needed 100 percent participation. The ACLU and Attorney John True of the Employment Law Center worked with the employees on the case and a restraining order was issued to halt the testing. It was one of the first tests of drug testing and right-to-privacy laws in California.

Hercules asserted that there was no reason to believe that there was a drug problem at the refinery. The decision to do the testing was made at the home office in Houston, because of a belief that drug use is "pretty pervasive" in society. True pointed out that the test in no way showed anything about impairment on the job, but it could indicate pregnancy or ingestion of legal medications, which would be an invasion of privacy.

The right of employers to test employees for drugs has evolved since wide spread testing began. Testing of strongly suspected drug users, crews involved in accidents, and personnel in sensitive positions has been upheld by the Supreme

Court. However, the fact is that most employees do not use drugs, do not have sensitive positions, and are not involved in serious accidents.

Justice Scalia was with the 7 to 2 Supreme Court majority upholding post-accident testing in *Skinner v. Railway Labor Executives Association.* He dissented from the narrow 5 to 4 majority upholding testing of some, but not all, Customs employees. Justice Scalia noted that only five of 3,600 Customs employees tested positive for drugs. Of the 30,000 Federal employees tested in 1988 under the random spot checking program only 203 tested positive, a rate of less than 0.7 percent.

The Supreme Court seems to be shifting in its interpretation of the Fifth Amendment away from the negative requirement of "particularized" suspicion for reasonable searches. Civil libertarians warn about such erosion of privacy, primarily of the innocent. They say this shift prepares the way for dragnet office searches, blanket AIDS testing, or regular searches of travelers. Contrasting the documented record of alcohol and drug abuse among railroad workers with the data on Customs workers, Justice Scalia wrote that there is no "real evidence of a real problem that will be solved" by drug testing. He added, "Symbolism, even symbolism for so worthy a cause as the abolition of unlawful drugs, cannot validate an otherwise unreasonable search."

Given the narrow 5 to 4 vote and limited scope of the Supreme Court decision in *National Treasury Employees Union* v. *Von Raab,* it is likely that there will be limits to drug testing. Responding to the Court's decision, Dr. Michael Walsh of NIDA, National Institute on Drug Abuse, said, "The issue in our program has always been who (to test). The most difficult decision is where to draw the line. Nuclear people are obviously in, and clerical people are obviously out, but there are a lot of people in the middle."

Voluntary Consent

Due process can be demonstrated when you actually consent to the test. Of course, consent must be voluntary, not forced. There is debate over this issue, because people naturally wonder whether consent is genuinely free if the possibility of being fired is implicit in refusing.

Even when reasonable suspicion or probable cause exist, an employer should never attempt to forcibly extract a sample from you—which could be considered to be a form of battery. In one such incident, UPS was sued because a company nurse demanded that an employee, who had been a drug user and had been through a drug treatment program, provide immediate samples of his blood and urine for testing when he returned from vacation. When the employee objected, the nurse disregarded his protest and "plunged a needle into his arm and extracted blood." Such a use of force constitutes blatant violation of principles of privacy and consent. Samples should always be obtained with your consent only.

You Should Be Informed

Informing you and your co-workers, either in your handbook or by placing notices on bulletin boards, about the drug testing program, how it will work, and what the sanctions will be taken for positive results is how most companies get around consent and demonstrate that you have been treated fairly.

Prior Notification And Consent

The Department of Justice has taken the position that when a public employee is told that drug testing is a condition of employment and *does not quit*, this is in fact consent to the testing. Interesting logic! The Courts have supported the idea that voluntary consent to a search satisfies requirements of the Fourth Amendment.

> *"A valid consent to a search must in fact be voluntarily given, and not be the result of duress or coercion, expressed or implied. It flies in the face of economic reality to suppose that an employee voluntarily consents to a drug test when the alternative is losing his or her job, or, for that matter, that an applicant voluntarily consents when the alternative is being denied the job. Agreement to a search motivated by fear that refusal will lead to loss of one's livelihood is not voluntary consent."*
>
> Office of the Attorney General
> Maryland

Voluntary consent cannot necessarily be inferred from your decision to accept a job with the knowledge that drug testing is a condition of that job. In both *McDonnell* v. *Hunter* and *Security and Law Enforcement Employees* v. *Carey,* the prison employees were told at the onset of their employment that they would be subject to certain searches. In the McDonnell case, the employees actually signed a consent form expressing their agreement, among other things, to submit to a urinalysis or blood test when requested by the prison administrator. In the Carey case, they were given a rule book which stated that any employee on duty would be subject to a search. Nevertheless, the Court held that neither circumstance gave rise to voluntary consent. In both cases, the Courts ruled that it was coercion and not consent. If the choice to decline the search carries with it significant adverse consequences, then the alternative, submitting to the search, does not reflect voluntary consent.

"Consent" in any meaningful sense cannot be said to exist merely because you (a) know that an official intrusion into your privacy is contemplated if you do a certain thing, and then (b) you proceed to do that thing. Were it otherwise, the police could, for instance, use the implied-consent theory to subject everyone on the street after 11 p.m. to physical search, merely by making public announcements in the press, radio, and television that such searches would be undertaken.

Two Views

We're convinced that under the circumstances, this test will be proved to be Constitutional. We're in a situation . . . where the country has a real serious problem on its hands. And I think, under the circumstances, a drug testing program is appropriate. Let me try to draw a parallel. A number of years ago, we used to be able to get on airplanes and fly from city to city without going through magnetometers and having our baggage searched at the gate. We developed a serious problem. We couldn't take an airplane flight without ending up in Cuba. We had to put in a fairly comprehensive program in our airports to stop this from happening, and the Courts, when weighing the problem against the intrusion in one's personal life, decided this was Constitutional.

Stephen Trott
Justice Department

If the government were to announce that all telephones would be hereafter tapped, perhaps to counter an outbreak of political kidnappings, it would not justify, even after public knowledge of the wiretapping plan, the proposition that anyone using a telephone consented to being tapped. It would not matter that other means of communication exist . . . it is often a necessity of modern living to use a telephone. So also it is often a necessity to fly on a commercial airliner, and to force one to choose between that necessity and the exercise of a Constitutional right is coercion in the Constitutional sense.

U.S. v. *Albarado*

The question of whether or not testing is voluntary is very important, because a valid voluntary consent excuses the need for a warrant or for probable cause prior to testing. In a private business setting, an employment policy posted publicly is generally taken to mean that all of the employees have consented to the policy. However, this may not be legally valid. A lawsuit (*Luck* v. *Southern Pacific*) in California was filed by a pregnant woman named Barbara Luck who worked for the company for six years as a computer programmer and refused to take an unannounced test administered to everyone in her department. Luck was fired because she did not consent to the test. She sued for wrongful termination. The jury was instructed that Southern Pacific had to show that it was "necessary" to test Luck "in order to achieve the public interest of safety in the operation and maintenance of the railroad." Southern Pacific failed to prove necessity and the jury awarded $485,000 to Luck in a unanimous verdict.

Southern Pacific appealed the ruling. In the Spring of 1990 a Court of Appeal decision upheld the jury award in favor of Barbara Luck. The California State Appeal Court ruled that employers must have a "compelling interest" when asking their workers to submit to random drug tests if the employees are not in safety-sensitive positions. The ruling applies to all California employers, public and private. However, it does not speak to the issue of testing job applicants. The "compelling interest" requirement for a person already employed is more stringent than the existing requirement used for job applicants. Applicants may be tested if the employer's right to know outweighs the applicant's right to privacy. Luck's attorney summaried by saying, "By this decision, employers (in California) must exercise extreme caution before they require any employee to submit to any test as a condition of employment."

CHAPTER 9

What About Prescription Drugs And Addictions?

The Courts have ruled that drug testing is a search—a search of your urine, blood or hair. In the process of such a search your lawful prescription drug use could be revealed. You are asked to disclose your drug use. And, as in the case of a positive test result, you must do so in order to explain lawful drug use, which might be to treat a disability. Once this information is known it could be used to discriminate against you by denying employment on the basis of the disability, when you are otherwise qualified to do the job. This is a serious problem because it could violate your civil rights. In 1990 the American Disabilities Act (ADA) was enacted to protect you if you are disabled.

The American Disabilities Act, which applies to government agencies and employers with 15 or more employees, expanded equal employment law by creating a new "protected class" of Americans—individuals with disabilities— estimated to include 43 million people, or about one-sixth of the population of the United States.

Psychological disorders, such as depression and schizophrenia, are defined as disabilities, along with alcoholism and drug addiction. If you have a psychiatric diagnosis and are taking prescribed psychiatric drugs under the supervision of an appropriate health professional, your drug use is protected under the ADA. Testing for prescription drugs and probing into your medical information to uncover the use of such drugs is prohibited, because this information could be used to discriminate if you're disabled. This same protection extends to recovered or recovering alcoholics and drug addicts because they are disabled. The ADA does not protect individuals currently using illicit drugs or using prescription drugs illegally, however. These behaviors are specifically exclused from coverage.

Past vs Present Drug Use

The ADA makes a distinction between past and present drug use, and between legal and illegal prescription drug use. Illicit drug use in *the past* by a *drug addict* is considered a disability and protected; whereas *current* illicit drug use is not considered a disability and is not protected by the ADA. Illicit drug use in the past by a casual user who was *not* addicted is not protected because causal drug use is not considered a disability. Use of a prescription drug under the supervision of an appropriate health care professional is legal drug use and protected, however. Improper use of a prescription drug is illegal and not protected by the ADA.

If you're a recovering alcoholic or drug addict, employers are prohibited from considering your *former* drug or alcohol abuse when hiring you, because alcoholism and drug addiction are defined as disabilities by the ADA. Asking you about your *former* drug or alcohol use, including addiction or treatment, during a job interview is a violation of the ADA and can be the basis for a discrimination suit—even if you are subsequently hired. On the other hand, asking you about *current* use of illicit drugs during a job interview is permitted, because such use is illegal and not protected by the ADA.

Questions That Companies Cannot Ask During Job Interview

What prescription drugs do you use?
Have you ever abused drugs or alcohol?
Have you ever been in drug or alcohol treatment?
Are you an addict or alcoholic?
Have you ever been arrested for driving under the influence (DUI)?

Questions That Companies Are Permitted To Ask During Job Interview

Do you drink?
Do you currently use illegal drugs?
Have you used marijuana in the last 30 days?
Have you ever been convicted of a DUI?
Have you ever had your driver's license suspended or revoked?
Have you ever been convicted of a felony related to drug or alcohol use?

What is Current Use?

The ADA does not clearly define current versus past use. Current use is not limited to the use of drugs on the day of, or within a matter of days or weeks before, the drug test. The Equal Employment Opportunity Commission (EEOC) has clarified it as "the illegal use of drugs that has occurred recently enough to indicate that the individual is actively engaged in such conduct." This includes current known on-the-job use and job impairment due to illicit drug use. It also includes a positive urine drug test which is equated with current usage. Past drug use is generally considered to be use prior to six months in the past.

While the time distinction between current and past is not fixed, "current" is supposed to be broad enough that, if you get a positive drug test, it precludes you from claiming that you have a disability—and are thereby protected from discipline—by running out and enrolling in a rehabilitation program. In practice, however, immediately signing up for rehab could be an astute move.

Employers are allowed to test you for drugs if you are disabled, provided they are testing for current illicit drug use and disabled people as a class are not singled out for the testing. That is, abled and disabled alike are tested. Employers are not allowed to test for prescription drugs, except when you are believed to be using prescription drugs improperly, such as taking someone else's prescription, in which case it is illegal drug use.

Drug Addiction Is A Disability

It is a violation of the ADA to discriminate against recovering drug addicts and alcoholics. "Recovering" is defined as participating in or having successfully completed a supervised drug rehabilitation program and no longer using drugs illegally. This doesn't mean that employers must hire you if you are a drug addict. That would be absurd. But rejecting you solely on the basis of drug addiction or alcoholism is illegal. The law does allow for exceptions, however. A person who is not currently using drugs but who has a history of drug abuse can be fired or refused employment in certain occupations such as law enforcement, for example, when it can be demonstrated that the prohibition is job-related and a business necessity.

The American Disabilities Act also protects people who are erroneously regarded as using drugs illegally. For example, suppose that based upon a rumor, which turned out to be false, your supervisor believed you were a drug addict using illegal drugs. You would be protected by the ADA and regarded as an individual with a disability. On the other hand, if the supervisor did not think you were an addict but simply using illegal drugs recreationally, you would not be regarded as an individual with a disability and would not be protected by the ADA.

In other words, employers are prohibited from rejecting your application and taking adverse action against you on the basis of a disability, even when that disability is drug addiction. Employers are permitted, however, to not hire and to fire or otherwise discipline employees who are shown to be currently using illicit drugs or illegally using prescription drugs.

Medical Examinations

Under the ADA employees and job candidates with disabilities have enhanced privacy protection for medical information. Employers cannot probe into your medical history or legal use of prescribed drugs—except when there is a genuine safety or health reason for doing so—because knowing this information could be used to discriminate against you. Since alcoholism and drug addiction are considered disabilities under the law, employers are restricted as to when and how they can probe into your past alcohol and drug use. This includes urine testings, reviews of positive drug tests by a company's Medical Review Officer, and questions asked during interviews.

Urine testing for alcohol use is defined by the ADA as a medical examination and restricted, whereas drug testing to detect the use of illegal drugs is not a medical examination and is permitted, provided it is applied to abled and disabled alike. The distinction in the law was made because alcohol consumption is legal and the use of illicit drugs is not.

The ADA states that a medical examination of a disabled job applicant can only be performed *after* an offer of employment and *before* the employee begins employment duties—and only if required of *all* entering employees. During this brief window the employer can administer a drug test for alcohol use without violating the American Disabilities Act. Urine testing for illegal drugs, on the other hand, is not defined as a medical examination under the ADA which means that drug testing of job applicants is permitted as long as it is applied uniformly and not just to disabled applicants.

If you are disabled and, in the course of applying for a job, get a positive drug test, things get even more complicated. Because some positive tests results have a legitimate explanation, such as having taken a prescribed medication, normally you would be asked to meet with the company Medical Review Officer (MRO) to discuss the result and provide your explanation for the positive result. Under the ADA such a meeting is considered a "medical examination" and prohibited, except after extending a job offer to you. In order words, it is legal to perform a pre-offer drug test, but it is not legal to perform a pre-offer MRO inquiry about a positive result—a requirement of Mandatory Federal Guidelines. To avoid getting caught in this Catch-22 many employers do drug testing after extending the job offer, but before you begin working.

Testing for Alcohol

Testing for alcohol, unlike testing for use of illegal drugs, is defined as a medical examination under the ADA. This means that all of the requirements and restrictions applying to medical examinations apply to testing for alcohol. Alcohol testing can *only* be performed post-offer and pre-employment. Stated in another way, employers can test for alcohol only after they have offered you a job and only if the offer is conditioned upon the test results.

To further complicate matters, a positive alcohol test alone is not a sufficient basis for denying employment, except for safety-sensitive jobs. This is because use of alcohol is legal and you may be a recovered or recovering alcoholic—which is a disability protected by the ADA. Whether or not an employer can take action against you because of a positive alcohol test will depend upon the particulars of your situation. To deny you work on the basis of alcohol use, the employer has to have a broader basis of evidence than simply a positive test result. The employer might try to demonstrate that you cannot perform the essential functions of the job and are therefore not qualified. Another approach is to show that the use of alcohol is likely to pose a "direct threat to the health or safety of others in the workplace". Thirdly, the employer might demonstrated that you are not actually a recovered or recovering alcoholic and therefore not disabled and thus not protected by the ADA. Finally, employers can take adverse action against you if you violate posted company policy such as "no drinking on the job", so long as the rules are applied to all employees equally.

If you have the misfortune of getting a positive drug test and you have been through a treatment program or are currently in one, you may experience violations of your rights under the American Disabilities Act. Once again, the astute action is to keep detailed notes on your experience—who said what to whom when. These will be invaluable if this disagreeable situation should expand into litigation.

Prescription Drugs

The ADA explicitly protects your lawful use of prescription drugs. If your employer pries into your use of prescription drugs and you end up in Court suing, it will probably be presumed that your employers' interest was discriminatory and had a disparate impact on the disabled—you—unless a compelling "business necessity" for such prying can be demonstrated. In the early days of drug testing employers often required job applicants and employees to report their use of prescription drugs. This type of blanket disclosure requirement is not likely to withstand a legal challenge. There is a loophole: health and safety—that is, when the use of prescription drugs may cause impairment that could lead to dangerous situations. The employer must prove that such medical inquiries are job-related and consistent with business necessity.

Exceptions

There are two exceptions to the rule that an employer cannot discriminate against you if you are disabled. If you were a recovered drug addict an employer can refuse to hire you if it can show that the decision is job-related and consistent with business necessity. An employer might refuse to place you in a position where you could pose a threat to the health or safety if you suffered a relapse. If you were an alcoholic, an employer could discharge, discipline or deny employment to you if your use of alcohol adversely affected your job performance to the extent that you are not longer qualified to perform the job.

Employers can prohibit you from using drugs and alcohol while at work, or from coming to work under the influence of drugs and alcohol. If you violate your company's drug-free workplace rules you could be disciplined or discharged without violating the ADA. Similarly, substance abusing disabled employees may be held to the same standard of conduct and performance that the company demands of non-disabled employees.

CHAPTER 10

Be Prepared

If you work for a Fortune 500 Company, the Federal or State government, hold a "sensitive position" such as a schoolteacher, or drive a truck, you will face a drug test sooner or later. Professional athletes and people preparing to adopt children face drug testing. In fact, in this day and age of Big Brother, just about everyone has to worry about a urine inspection.

Obviously your primary objective is to pass the test. Don't think that just because you are a straight arrow and don't do drugs that you're safe. Wrong! Even if you use no illegal drugs at all you can still get a positive drug test. Then your silly goose is cooked—based, roasted and served up on a platter! If you've taken an over-the-counter medicine for a cold you can test like a druggie. Or maybe you've eaten a poppy seed bagel. Well, the test can say that you're an opium user! Or maybe you've passively inhaled your roommate's pot smoke. Well, that can give you a positive read, too. Or maybe the lab tech will screw up. The fact is just because you're a good kid and keep your nose (and pee) clean, you can't sit on your laurels. You *could* get a positive drug test. And if you do use illegal drugs, *they're looking for you, babe!* So you'd better get prepared.

Preparing For The Test

Be proactive. Get prepared. Don't make the mistake of waiting until the results are in before taking action. Educating yourself in advance is vital both for devising a strategy to pass the test and for being prepared to respond effectively to a positive result—if you're faced with *that* bummer! If you're smart you'll educate yourself *now!* Don't even wait until you're scheduled for testing. Find out about drug testing in general and the company's program and policies in particular.

The first step is to find out as much as possible about what tests are going to be given. Depending on which test is used, a different strategy for passing the test will be called for. The test most commonly given is a relatively crude screening test, such as the EMIT® or RIA. Screening tests give a "yes or no" answer that says that a drug metabolite—a chemical residue of drugs—have been detected in your urine. It does not identify the specific substance responsible for the positive result. Screening test are particularly problematic because over-the-counter drugs can cross-react to generate a positive result without your having taken any illicit substances.

Screening tests are often given to job applicants. If you're tested in the course of applying for a job and get a positive result, you'll probably never know it. You just don't get hired, that's all! And who knows where the record of that result is stored—or who has access to it. This is particularly unfair if the positive result is due to the cross-reactivity of an over-the-counter medicine. You are never given the opportunity to demonstrate your innocence. So there's plenty of reason to think about protecting yourself. It's already a dog-eat-dog world out there; you don't need the additional hassle of a positive drug testing screwing up your existence

You might be in a situation, such as a government agency or work in the transportation industry, for example, where random drug testing is used to keep people drug-free through fear of being detected. Here again, the objective is to get a general "yes or no" answer. So screening tests are used in random testing. If your pee comes up positive, then it'll be tested again with a more sophisticated test that can confirm the result and tell what you've been taking. The scary thing about random testing is that it reveals legal prescription drug use right along with illegal use. Maybe you don't want your boss to know that you're taking Prozac® or Viagra®! This snooping in your bodily fluids can tell a lot of your secrets, like being pregnant, for example. Maybe you just want privacy. Here's another reason to be concerned about taking a pee test.

Regularly scheduled drug tests can be demanded of people on probation and in treatment programs. Once again, the intent is control and monitoring. Regular testing helps recovering drug addicts stay clean. It could be the price for getting probation instead of jail time. Inexpensive drug screens that give a "yes or no" result are usually used in this situation.

Other times a drug test is given in response to a particular circumstance, such as an accident investigation or a criminal proceeding. In these situations the test used is more sensitive and can detect smaller concentrations of drug metabolites and identify what drug is responsible for the positive result. Gas chromatography/mass spectrometry (GC/MS) is the test most commonly used for such purposes.

Companies and rehab facilities rarely use this expensive, more sensitive testing method except for confirmation of a positive. Confirmations are suppose to be done by more sophisticated testing methodology. But this rule can be ignored and a second screening-type test can be used to confirm the positive result from the initial screening test. This is a lot cheaper, but it's cheating. If this happens to you, you need to know enough to have your lawyer protest and demand that your initial positive test be properly confirmed. Let's hope you never find yourself in this defensive situation. Start by being informed.

Where To Get Information

One way to get information is by asking questions of the right people. Supervisors and other employees who have already been tested can be sources of relevant information. Finding out from co-workers the step-by-step procedures they went through is helpful in preparing to be tested. Company announcements are another available resource. The employee handbook should give disclosures about the company's testing program and how it works. Personnel officers can explain the procedures and provide additional information. Union stewards are another source you can consult. Unions have guidelines for handling the testing process, and inform their members about what pitfalls to avoid.

Another source of information is the drug test manufacturers themselves. Some of them have 800 phone numbers and most of them are on the Internet. Syva Company in Palo Alto, California has a national toll-free number (800-227-8994). Roche Diagnostic Systems, located in New Jersey, also has a toll-free number (800-526-1247). These companies will send packets of information and respond to inquiries.

Avoid Suspicion

When making inquiries, a subtle manner will help prevent needless suspicion. Asking a lot of questions about drug tests might give your supervisor or some snitch reason to wonder why. Prepare responses for comments like, "Well, why are you asking all these questions? Do you have something to be worried about?" Knowing in advance how you will answer such questions will help to reduce defensiveness. The best approach is to emphasize how much you value the job. For example, you might say, "I've read that there are a lot of errors on these tests, and my job is important to me. I want to make sure I understand what's going on so there won't be any screw-ups."

tested, and requires the issuance of a written report on the incident. If you're contemplating refusing to give a sample it is advisable to consult with an attorney before the fact rather than afterward.

The Consent Form typically has the name of the company performing the test and the employer (in cases when these are different), the date, and your name, job title, and ID number. You will be asked to sign a statement that the information given is complete and correct. Typically it says that you understand that the urine sample is going to be analyzed to determine the presence of illicit drugs and alcohol and that you are aware that the results will be given to your employer. You can legitimately request that the test result be kept confidential from all other parties.

Refusing To Be Tested

Yes, you can refuse to give consent, but if you do, you can kiss your job good-bye. No matter what reason you give for not wanting to be tested, you will be suspect. For example, San Francisco Giants outfielder Joel Youngblood refused to be tested. What? You never heard of him? Well, that's because he terminated his career when he refused to be tested. He was squeaky-clean in the drug department. Yet because he balked at including a drug testing clause in his contract, he became baseball's unwanted man.

What irked Youngblood was the proviso that the Giants could test for drugs at anytime, day or night, as often as they liked. "It puts you in the position of having to prove your innocence," his agent said. "It's like having the police coming to your house at 3 a.m. just to look around. No reason."

During the winter Youngblood's agent worked out the details of the next year's contract. But when he held off on the drug testing clause, the Giants withdrew their offer. No one else in the league would touch Youngblood, either. Suddenly, the nine-year veteran became baseball's untouchable.

Shy Bladder

Occasionally, a person is unable to pee because he or she either urinated recently or has a "shy" bladder. Generally, the term refers to an individual who is unable to provide a sufficient specimen either upon demand or when someone is nearby. The Collector is required to keep records of each attempted urination. If this happens to you, you will be given large quantities of fluids, such as 8 ounces every 30 minutes up to 24 ounces in 2 hours. If you cannot pee into your little bottle you will probably be reported as "refusing" to provide a sample.

Disclosure

You will also be asked to "disclose" what medications or drugs you have been taken in the past week. Usually the form requests that you write down the name of the medication, the reason for having taken it, how much was taken, when it was prescribed, and who prescribed it. You will be asked to sign the disclosure.

Nightbyrd, in his underground classic, *Conquering The Urine Tests*, suggests that you cross out "7 days" and write in "30 days," because many common substances stay in the body much longer than seven days. He also suggests you be prepared to be questioned for making this or any other changes on the form. If you are asked why you are worried about the test, for example, Nightbyrd suggests that you have a prepared answer, such as stating that you value their job and you've heard of false positives where drug-free employees have tested positive and been fired. So you are just being cautious in writing down anything that you have taken in the last 30 days. Nightbyrd also suggests you write your own disclaimer in your own language at the bottom of the form, such as, "This list is my best recollection. There may have been other legal medications or substances that I taken which I don't remember at this time." Such a disclaimer could be helpful if you test positive and have to pursue a legal remedy.

Disclose Cross-Reactants

Employees who use recreational drugs often disclose over-the-counter or prescribed remedies that can cause positive test results for the drugs they've been using. This becomes a potential loophole if they test positive.

If a positive is revealed, you can point to the Disclosure Form where the over-the-counter or prescription substance was indicated. Of course, the Medical Review Officer, who reviews positive results before reporting them to the company, will probably schedule a confirmatory test which will be more specific about which metabolite was in your urine. Nonetheless, disclosure of the cross-reactant before the first test will provide your attorney with some leverage in the situation, should it escalate into the legal arena.

Cross-Reactivity

Positive for	Cross-Reactivity	Examples
Marijuana	Ibuprofen	Advil®, Nuprin®
Amphetamines	Phenypropanolamine	Diatec®, Dexatrim® Cotylenol®, Triaminic®
	Ephedrine	Primatene®, Bronkotabs® Nyquil®
Opiates	Dextromethorphan	Vicks Formula 44-M®
	Amitripyline	Elavil®
	Meperidine	Demarol®
	Imprimine	Tofranil®
	Perylamine	Mydol®, Permensin®
Barbiturate	Phenobarbital	Primatene®
Methadone	Diphenhydramine	Benadryl®

Source: Abbie Hoffman, *Steal This Urine Test*

Getting A Legal Prescription

An alternative strategy is obtaining a legal prescription from a sympathetic doctor for the substance you may taken or for a substance that has a positive cross-reactivity for what you've been taking. That prescription is then disclosed on the form. For example, Hoffman suggests that a doctor may prescribe a codeine-based cough syrup to an employee who has been using opiates. If an opiate has been used, the cough syrup can be ingested before the test, and also disclosed on the form, stating that it was used recently. The doctor is then available to substantiate that there is a legal prescription for a drug that could be responsible for the positive result.

Some employees have been able to find sympathetic doctors by asking pharmacists for referrals. Obviously, during such questioning the person looking for a "script doctor" must be very subtle in the inquiry. For example, "I've just moved here and I wonder if you could help me find a good doctor. My old doctor prescribed me thus-and-such each month for thus-and-such problems. Would you know of a good doctor around here who works with people with problems like mine?"

On the other hand, it may not be wise to disclose certain medications, even when you have a legal prescription and valid reasons for taking it. Disclosing your use of a psychiatric drug may cause your employer to wonder if you suffer from a mental illness. Of course, you would probably be considered "disabled" under the American Disabilities Act, in which case it's illegal for your employer to entertain such suspicions. But realistically, being in the "right" doesn't help. Suspicions are suspicions.

Many companies have policies which do not allow use of any drug that could have side effects affecting job performance, whether prescribed or not. In that case you would be required to disclose lawful medications. If you are taking a legally prescribed behavior-altering drug, including sleeping pills or drugs for epilepsy, it might be advisable to meet with a doctor—and in some cases with an attorney—before taking the test and before filling out the disclosure form.

Sending Results Your Own Physician

It is also permissible to request that information about the testing methods be sent to your doctor. This request could be written on the consent form, thus becoming part of the conditions of consent to testing. If you come up with a positive result, the doctor may be able to provide information that will explain a false positive result, such as using a particular prescribed medication.

The Split Sample

Employees who are absolutely drug-free can still come up with false positives due to clerical errors or failures in chain-of-custody procedures. It's smart to take steps in advance to protect against this possibility. One form of insurance is to insist on a split sample. One-half of the sample is sent to the company's testing lab, and the other half is refrigerated or frozen. If the lab results indicate a positive for a drug, the remaining sample can be split again and one-half sent to the company's lab for retesting, and the other half to a knowledgeable lawyer to arrange for an independent testing at a different lab. This provides legal evidence if you are unfairly accused. This strategy is advised in situations where testing is a result of an "incident," such as an accident or accused drug use.

Custody and Control Form

Before they were standardized, chain of custody forms became a nightmare because employers used different forms. This problem was corrected with rules which mandate the use of an approved Custody and Control Form (CCF), to be used to document the collection of a specimen at the collection site. The OMB-approved (Office of Management and Budget) CCF is usually supplied by the testing lab. The OMB-approved CCF may not be modified. The *Urine Specimen Collection Handbook for Federal Workplace Drug Testing Programs* can be ordered from the National Clearinghouse for Alcohol and Drug Information (NCADI) and is available at the NCADI website (www.health.org/workpl.htm).

CHAPTER 12

Strategy: Abstaining

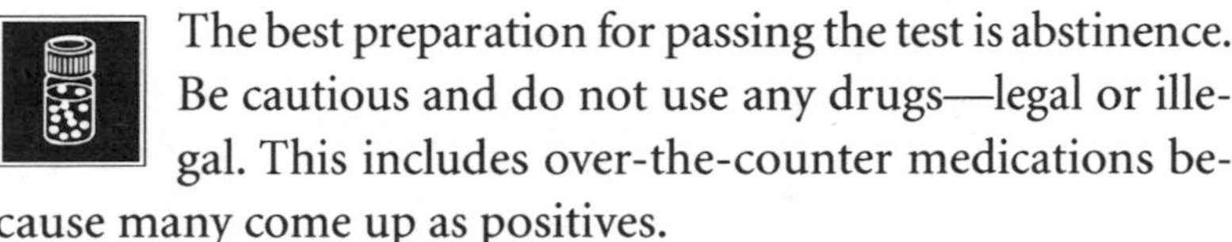

The best preparation for passing the test is abstinence. Be cautious and do not use any drugs—legal or illegal. This includes over-the-counter medications because many come up as positives.

However, false positives are still possible even if you use no drugs at all. For example, there could be a lab screw up. A food you've eaten could cause a positive. Or there could be something in your biology that reads positive. If you get a false positive it'll cast suspicion on you and you'll be subjected to further testing and examination. This fact is particularly alarming given that your livelihood and reputation are probably at stake.

Avoid Over-The Counter Medicines

If you've used a perfectly legal medicine from the drugstore to soothe your flu symptoms and you are tested for drugs, there is a high probability that you will test positive for speed or opiates—or both. The government is aware of this kind of false positive—false because you tested positive when you had not used any illicit drug—and built a supposed fail-safe into the drug testing program architecture to deal with it. You are given the opportunity to disclose legal medicines you've taken on the paperwork you complete when tested and you will be questioned by the Medical Review Officer about possible reasons for the result. If the MRO buys your story he or she can report a positive as a negative and your company will never know.

But who wants the hassle, stress and suspicion? It is much better to never get that false positive in the first place! One way to reduce the odds of a positive result is to avoid over-the-counter-medicines that cause positive results.

Over-The-Counter Medications To Avoid

Alka-Seltzer Plus®
Allerest®
Bronkaid®
Contac®
Donnagel®
Nyquil®
Primatene®
Sinutab®
Sudafed®
Triaminic®

Detection Periods

If you have been using drugs and you plan to clean up to pass the test, you'll need to abstain long enough for the metabolites to work their way through your system. The length of time a drug metabolite can be found in bodily fluids is known as the "detection period". Detection periods vary widely according to the inherent physical and chemical properties of the drug itself, your history of use, and your age, sex, body weight, and health. For example, the cocaine detection period is very short (12 to 48 hours), whereas marijuana has a longer detection period, depending on drug-use history. Casual marijuana use can be detected from 2 to 7 days later; with chronic use, detection could be as long as two months after the last use. On the other hand, a single puff of low potency marijuana may be undetectable after 12 hours.

The duration of the abstinence necessary to come up negative varies because different drugs are metabolized and excreted by the body at different rates. The table shows the time periods after which the drugs listed are reported to become undetectable as reported by PharmChem, a leading testing facility in Menlo Park, California.

PharmChem's Drug Detection Periods For Urine

Drug	Detection Period
Amphetamines—Stimulants	
Amphetamine	Up to 72 hours
Methamphetamine	Up to 72 hours
Barbiturates—Sedative Hypnotics	1-4 days
Amobarbital	2-4 days
Butalbital	2-4 days
Pentobarbital	2-4 days
Phenobarbital	Up to 30 days
Secobartial	2-4 days
Bensodiazepines—Sedative Hypnotics	
Diazepam (Valium)	Up to 30 days
Chlordiazepoxide (Librium)	Up to 30 days
Cannabinoids—Euphoriants	
Marijuana	
Casual use	1-4 days
Chronic use	Up to 14 days*
Cocaine—Stimulants	
Benzoylecgorine	Up to 72 hours
Ethanol—Sedative Hypnotics	
Alcohol	Very short**
Methadone—Narcotic Analgesics	1-4 days
Methaqualone—Sedative Hypnotics	
Quaalude	2-4 days
Opiates—Narcotic Analgesic	
Codine	2-4 days
Hydromorphone	2-4 days
Morphine for Heroin	2-4 days
Phencyclidine (PCP)—Hallucinogens	
Casual use	Up to 5 days
Chronic use	Up to 14 days*

* In rare cases, an individual may be at a detectable level for up to 30 days. **Alcohol is excreted at the rate of approximately one oz. per hour.

Individual Differences

The length of time for which drug metabolites are retained by the body can vary dramatically from person to person. Relevant factors include your weight, fat level, and speed of metabolism, as well as the frequency and duration of your drug use and the dosages involved. According to Dr. John Morgan, Medical Professor and Director of the Pharmacology Program at the City University of New York, one heavy marijuana smoker who was incarcerated continued to secrete the acid metabolite for more than two months. PharmChem, on the other hand, claims positives for marijuana after a month of abstinence is rare. Still if you're a stoner you'll want to sit up and take notice. While you're indulging in one of the most benign drugs, less dangerous than cigarettes and most other drugs, marijuana use is the easiest detected—and the hardest to beat. It's an unfair world, so be prepared.

Testing Sensitivity

The length of the detection period depends on the sensitivity of the test used. The EMIT® has two cutoff sensitivities, high and low. The low cut-off level detects a concentration of about one fifth of the high level. Knowing more about the sensitivity of the test used helps to determine how long to abstain. But the rule of thumb is: When in doubt, go without! Some people call in sick to get in an extra day of abstinence—which itself can arouse suspicion.

CHAPTER 13

Strategy: Flushing

The faster metabolites move through your system, the sooner you're clean and have reduced the danger of testing positive. With the flushing strategy, you put as much liquid through your system as possible, to wash drug metabolites out of your body. Removal of 100 percent of the metabolites in your system is unlikely, but flushing can dramatically reduce the concentration of metabolites in your urine sample.

At the request of the Department of Transportation (DOT) Office of Drug Enforcement, researcher Dr. Edward Cone of the Addiction Research Center (ARC) investigated the effectiveness of flushing. The government had read the underground literature on how to beat the test and was concerned about claims that certain herbal teas could be used to cleanse the system of drug metabolites. Cone's research showed that all it takes is drinking water!

Cone showed that when one gallon of water was drunk, not only did specific gravity fall to very low levels (specific gravity <1.003; creatinine<20), but the marijuana assay turned negative and stayed that way, even after specific gravity level had returned to normal. The cocaine tests turned negative for a few hours, but then turned positive again. The same results were observed whether or not tea was used (as compared to drinking plain water), When diuretics were taken, however, the test for both cannabinoids and cocaine turned negative and stayed that way, according to Cone's report in the American Academy of Forensic Sciences.

With the flushing strategy, when you know you are going to be tested you drink large quantities of water and other non-alcoholic liquids beginning one or two days before and during the morning of the test. It's not illegal to drink water, after all! Probably anyone facing a drug test should do so—just as a little insurance against a false positive. Stack the odds in your favor.

Your First Void Is The Dirtiest

Never give a sample from the first urine in the morning after waking from sleep, which is called the "first void" because it has the highest concentration of metabolites. In his book, *Steal This Urine Test,* Abbie Hoffman suggests not sleeping the night before testing or getting up earlier than usual in order to provide an opportunity for a greater number of urinations, each of which will further empty your body of metabolites in the hours before the test.

During any particular urination, the first part of your pee has the most metabolites. Some people advise pouring off the first half of the sample by peeing into the cup and pouring it into the toilet, then completing your pee into the cup. In this way, you throw away the portion of the pee containing the most metabolites.

Using Diuretics

Diuretics cause kidneys to step up the secretion of water. A *High Times Magazine* article suggested taking 80 milligrams of Lasix and increasing water intake in order to urinate two or three times before giving the sample. Furosemide, which is the generic name for Lasix, is a prescription drug, but not a controlled one. Family physicians can sometimes be persuaded to give a prescription.

Folks who can't get furosemide have been known to drink large amounts of coffee, because caffeine is a mild diuretic. A person facing an unannounced test can do a quick flush by downing a couple cups of coffee. It's readily available and doesn't arouse suspicion. Once again, drinking coffee is completely legal. Other natural diuretics include cranberry juice, beer, iced tea, herbal teas, sodas and grapes.

The idea is to pee as much as possible to flush metabolites from your system before giving the sample. Flushing will reduce your reading but it will not eliminate all drug metabolites. It doesn't guarantee a negative result, but it helps.

Cautions

A danger in drinking large quantities of water is that the resulting diluted urine will be detected and arouse suspicion leading to your company requesting a repeat urine. Creatinine levels may be tested and show that you have been flushing your body. Holtorf, author of *UR-INE TROUBLE*, says that most labs are too busy to analyze the urine's gravity and creatinine levels, so diluted urine usually goes undetected. This is particularly true of pre-employment drug testing.

To combat the low creatinine problem, some people eat red meat, because it is suppose to boost creatinine levels. If you eat a lot of red meat for the 3 days prior to the test, Holtorf says that creatinine levels will probably be normal even though you've been drinking large amounts of water.

Another danger is that diuretics can be harmful to pregnant women, people with kidney dysfunction, and people with diabetes. So don't try this technique if you even think you have any of these conditions!

Specific Gravity

Specific gravity is a measure of the relative proportion of dissolved solids, such as salts, to the volume of the urine specimen. It indicates concentration or dilution of the specimen in terms of the ratio of the weight of urine/weight of water. Normal values range from 1.003 to 1.030, but are usually between 1.010 and 1.025. Diabetes and several renal diseases cause chronic low specific gravity, adrenal insufficiency, hepatic disease, congestive heart failure, or dehydration can be a cause of high specific gravity. Urines with specific gravity less than 1.003 are considered abnormally dilute.

Creatinine

Creatinine is a by-product of muscle metabolism and constantly excreted. Creatinine less than 20 mg/dl is caused by drinking large quantities of water shortly before testing or by adding water directly to the urine specimen. Overhydration, as it is technically called, will dilute the drug concentration, but will also result in a low creatinine. Drinking large quantities of water cannot completely dilute urine to water, as there is a physiological limit to overhydration. In fact, a person could become sick through electrolyte imbalance from overhydration.

If creatinine is found to be diluted, the lab may perform a specific gravity and a dipstick. TOXNET Laboratories reports a story about receiving a specimen that was a combination of apple juice and urine, just the right color. It was identified by smell as apple juice upon opening. It contained a dilute creatinine, but a high specific gravity due to the apple juice. It also contained a large amount of glucose, normally absent in non-diabetic persons, but no ketones. The absence of ketones eliminated the possibility of the donor being a diabetic.

This is illustrative of the how laboratories use testing to detect adulteration. Medical review officers receiving negative reports with low creatinine and specific gravity are alerted to the possibility of adulteration by overhydration and can request an observed collection. However, not all employers request these secondary tests. In these situations flushing your system by drinking a lot of water can help you to pass the test.

Color Your Urine Yellow

Consuming large quantities of liquid makes urine nearly colorless, and a conspicuously colorless sample can arouse suspicion. Taking Vitamin B complex for several days before the test helps correct this problem, since it imparts a deep yellow color to urine. Some well prepared employees carry vitamins with them all the time. It only takes a few hours after popping the vitamins for your pee to become a dark yellow color. Like drinking water, taking vitamins is legal and lots of "health nuts" carry little pills boxes in their purses and brief cases.

Flushing Out Pot

The problem with pot is that its metabolites are stored in the fat, which is the reason that the detection time is so much longer than for most other drugs. Some people try to burn fat in an attempt to flush the traces of marijuana use from their bodies. One of the newest techniques is using lecithin, available in health food stores, which breaks down stored fat and disperses it into the blood stream. There is considerable debate as to when one should start taking the lecithin.

Athletes and exercise buffs have an advantage because when they exercise they burn fat and the THC metabolites are released from the lipid tissues and dumped into the blood stream. Due to athletes' high metabolism rates, THC metabolites move through their systems significantly faster. Exercising between drug tests cleans metabolites from the system at a faster rate which lowers detection period. A word of caution: when you exercise and burn fat, metabolites stored in your fat are released into your urine, so it is important to stop exercising before test time.

CHAPTER 14

Strategy: Masking

Another completely legal strategy for beating the test is masking. With this technique you ingests a substance that masks or covers the presence of drug metabolites in your urine so that they're not detected by the drug test.

Street-lore cites many products that are claimed to rid urine of drugs, but these methods have questionable, if any, results. Goldenseal, cranberry juice, vinegar, and aspirin are sometimes mentioned. U-R-KLEAN is a commercially sold tea claimed to clean urine. A study of 50 herbal teas failed to support claims that they mask drugs in urine. If drinking herbal tea does have an impact on drug testing results it is most likely a result of the consumption of liquids which flush the system as described in the previous chapter.

According to Holtorf, author of *UR-INE TROUBLE*, the hudrastine and berberine in goldenseal decreases the urine THC concentration only when high concentrations of the herb is used. The problem is that the concentration required is too high to be obtained by taking goldenseal orally. There is no effective method to obtain a high enough goldenseal concentration in urine to alter the test.

Vitamin C

Researchers Schwarzhoff and Cody report that vitamin C can cause a false negative result for marijuana, amphetamines and barbiturates. Holtorf says that taking 8,000 to 10,000 mg of the vitamin 4 to 6 hours before the test, followed by a second dose 2 hours before testing will probably mask marijuana use.

Large doses of vitamin C acidifies urine which increases excretion of amphetamines, cocaine and phencyclidine. Utilizing this information, some people take vitamin C for several days before drug testing to eliminate these drugs from their system.

This strategy is tricky, however, because when vitamin C is taken *just before testing* by users of amphetamines, cocaine and phencyclidine, its propensity to increase excretion can actually increase metabolites of these drugs in urine, thereby increasing the likelihood of a positive test.

Other Masking Agents

Ingesting bicarbonate and antacids like Tums and Rolaids decrease the excretion of amphetamines, cocaine and PCP and reduce getting a positive test. Another masking agent is Tolmetin, a prescription NSAID (nonsteroidal anti-inflammatory drug) similar to ibuprofen. Research by Dr. Cone's team revealed some ability to hide cannabinoids and opioids in urine tests. Ciprofloxicin, a common antibiotic, may be able to hide opiates, cocaine, amphetamines and benzodiazepines on immunoassay tests.

meanor. If you live in Nebraska and are caught adding water to your urine sample you are likely to be charged. The Texas law makes it a crime to use a substance or device to falsify a drug test. Chances are if you are caught adding water to your urine sample in Texas, you will be facing a misdemeanor charge. You can be sure that more states will jump on the bandwagon by enacting similar anti-tampering laws.

The Dry Room

Besides using the bluing color, testing programs battle the problem of diluting the sample with what is called the "dry room". In a dry room, access to water is prevented so that it cannot be used for diluting samples. Water taps are sealed off and there is only a minimum of water in the toilet bowl (this water sometimes also contains a colored dye). Usually, the reservoir tank is also secured, so there's no access to clean water from that source.

Using Saline Solution

An approach that has been attempted with some success is the use of an IV (intravenous) saline bag. A 250cc intravenous solution bag can be taped under the arm. Such a bag can be purchased in some drug stores and most medical supply houses, usually without a prescription. Only pure saline solution can be safely used; other solutions may contain chemicals which can be detected, thereby revealing the dilution attempt.

Typically the bag is taped under the arm, where it stays warm, and the tube is taped down the front of the body to the pubic area. At the time of the test, a small amount of urine is put into the testing cup before the cup is filled by squeezing the saline fluid out of the bag. Usually the observer is on the other side of a partition, or stands behind the person giving the sample, and so cannot observe the tube easily.

This is a very risky procedure. If you try it and are caught you'll have a difficult time explaining why you have a bag of water tapped to your body. Not only will it be assumed that you do, indeed, have something to hide, but you'll probably feel pretty embarrassed and humiliated.

CHAPTER 16

Strategy: Substituting

If you use drugs illicitly you may become so terrified of getting a positive that you may want to try to substitute "clean" urine for your own. You may get it from a friend who you believe has been drug-free, or it may have come from a vendor of urine. Substitution is dangerous. Monitors are on the lookout. If you're caught, you could lose your job. If you're being tested for an insurance policy, the testing will probably take place in your own home or office, in which case substitution is pretty easy since you can prepare in advance. It's unlikely that the sample will be tested for temperature, for example. Substitution is also easy to accomplish when you are tested in a doctor's office because doctors are used to clinical testing where cheating is rarely a problem.

But substitution is fraud because you are giving someone else's pee and passing it off as yours. Fraud can carry stiff penalties. We (the authors and publisher) do not recommend that you commit fraud or otherwise break the law. However, this is a free society—or at least it is supposed to be free. You are permitted to have information that the government doesn't like. And you are permitted to do stupid things. Trying to pass off someone else's urine as yours is stupid because it is very risky and the consequences can be stiff.

Nightbyrd Clean Pee

In the late 1980s, Jeff Nightbyrd, operator of Byrd Laboratories, began by collecting and selling "clean pee". (Byrd Labs' address is P.O. Box 1441, Topanga, CA 90290.) Nightbyrd's first product was urine in its original liquid state, which sold for $49.95 a bag. He claimed to sell it for "experimental purposes only" (i.e., use by laboratories and scientists), and guaranteed that it was 100 percent pure urine. The urine was collected from a local Bible study group, tested, and then packed in plastic bags that included a tube through which it could be poured. But there were numerous problems with selling and transporting liquid urine, especially through the mail. For one thing, unrefrigerated urine has a shelf-life of under 18 hours.

An attempt at freeze-drying urine didn't work either. Subsequently, Nightbyrd laboratories offered a powdered urine, having the color and consistency of corn starch, which reconstituted with hot distilled water.

Getting Someone Else's Pee

Some people use a sample from a friend or relative. However, this has been a mistake for some people who failed to confirm the contributor's drug-use history. For example, there was the case of a professional man who smoked marijuana occasionally on the weekends and who was facing a drug test. Quite concerned, he asked one of his children for a urine sample, and felt confident going into the drug test. Imagine his surprise and humiliation when his test came up positive for cocaine!

How Samples Have Been Substituted

When the sample is given in a situation that is not observed and is relatively lax, such as a family doctor's office, substitution is simple. You simply go into the bathroom and put the substitute sample into the container. However, most testing is conducted in a testing facility at the place of employment, in testing labs, or in even more rigidly controlled court-monitored facilities. In these situations, if you attempt sample substituting you must be extraordinarily cautious.

Containers And Bags

Some people have used a catheter bag hidden under a shirt, with a tube running down a sleeve to deliver the bogus sample. This is risky. A body pat-down, or undressing to put on a gown, will reveal the bag—a discovery that would result in your being subjected to tighter testing procedures.

Pharmacy or hospital supply centers sell Bard Dispoz-a-Bag® Drainage Bags, the kind of bag used by ambulant patients. Typically, the bags are inexpensive and come in different sizes. Some sympathetic pharmacists and clerks in pharmacy supply stores may even offer advice as to how these products can be used for substituting urine.

Abbie Hoffman described using a large leg bag that allows for extra volume and is shaped in a way that makes it easy to hide around the middle of the body. He says that after the bag is filled with clean urine, the air should be squeezed out completely to minimize bulging and the bag sealed. A short piece of rubber tubing and a valve is be added for easy dispensing of the sample.

Hoffman says people can buy incontinence pants at a pharmacy or hospital supply store to help hold the bag in place. The bag is usually flattened on the skin around the abdomen. Once taped in place with surgical tape, the tube from the bag is brought down to the crotch. The valve tap is placed within easy reach, but hidden from sight. When the person gives the sample, the fluid flows down. People usually practice delivering the sample with water in the bag.

People hoping to substitute a sample usually use a bag taped to the body rather than attempting to carry the sample in a jar. If you are closely observed, the risk is higher, but motivated people have learned to hide the bag tube without being discovered.

Another approach that Hoffman described is the use of a reservoir-tipped, nonlubricating condom. He suggests filling one with the substitute sample and then putting a second condom over it, to prevent bursting, and taping it as close to the crotch as possible. When it is time to give the sample, he advised using a presharpened fingernail to puncture the tip. One woman filled a condom with a substitute urine and placed it inside her vagina. When it came time to deliver the sample, she used her fingernail to break the condom, and the urine flowed into the container as if it were her own. Some men have filled a condom with the substitute pee and then slipped it onto their penis, will the liquid in the end of the condom which is punctured when giving the sample.

People carrying a concealed container with a substitute urine in an observed situation have successfully avoided direct observation by claiming they just can't "go" when being watched. This is a common phenomenon which is referred to in the medical community as "shy bladder" or "blushing kidneys."

Dangers Of Substituting

Obviously, substituting is a high-risk strategy and not recommended. The best approach is abstinence combined with drinking a lot of liquids. However, if you are desperate enough to try this strategy do not substitute cat, dog, or other nonhuman urine, or try to manufacture fake urine by using water and artificial coloring. These attempts are watched for and easily detected.

Temperature

Some programs call for testing the temperature of the urine. If you plan to attempt a substitution you'd be smart to find out if they'll be testing for temperature. You need to know every step in the process. When Federal Guidelines are being followed, the temperature will be tested within four minutes of giving the sample, and if it is not within 90.5 to 99.8 degrees Fahrenheit, a new sample is to be taken, with the Collector directly watching you pee.

A sample that has been refrigerated in order to keep it fresh has to be warmed up before the test to avoid detection. Even if the temperature is not automatically measured, detection is still possible. If the sample seems unusually cold to the touch, it will probably then be subjected to temperature testing. One of the most effective methods used is holding the sample close to the body, where it will warm to your body temperature.

You Can Be Busted

Three states, Nebraska, Texas and Pennsylvania, have enacted criminal laws that punish those who seek to falsify drug testing results. On January 1998 it became a criminal act in Pennsylvania to sell, share, or use drug-free urine for evading or causing deceitful results on a drug test. Both the person providing the drug-free urine and the person using it, if caught and convicted, are looking at a misdemeanor of the third degree which is punishable by imprisonment for up to one year. If you are in Nebraska and you tamper with bodily fluids for the purpose of altering alcohol- or drug-test results, you are facing a Class I misdemeanor if caught and convicted. Legal prohibitions for manipulating drug tests are even broader in Texas, where its law states: "any person who knowingly or intentionally manufactures, delivers, owns, uses, or possesses, with intent, a substance or device designed to falsify drug test results is guilty of a misdemeanor."

CHAPTER 17

Strategy: Adulterating

Adulterating the sample by adding a substance that prevents it from testing positive is another high-risk strategy. It can work with careful preparation.

Salt

Probably the most common adulterant used is salt. Very little salt is required. The EMIT® test is most easily nullified by salt. Small quantities of lye, common table salt, or household ammonia neutralize the enzyme activity, ensuring a "no drug content" readout on the sample.

Trying salt on a confirmatory, highly sensitive test is unlikely to succeed. Thin-layer chromatographic (TLC) results are not affected by salt. Furthermore, manufacturers of drug tests warn employers about the use of salt. Many consultants advise that the pH factor of each urine sample be tested, because some contaminants push the pH factor of the sample outside the normal range for urine. If you are suspected of tampering with your sample you will be subjected to interrogation, suspicion and probably a second test with you being observed while you pee.

Sneaking Adulterants In

Some people have smuggled salt and other substances into the testing bathroom on their hands or under their fingernails. This won't work if the test is being conducted under the Federal Guidelines because you will be required to wash your hands and scrub your nails in the presence of a monitor. If the Federal Guidelines are not being followed, then you might be able to hide salt under the nails. However, making sure the salt will work can still be problematic.

When salt is put into a sample, it is vitally important that no crystals remain undissolved in the bottom of the container, since this will reveal the adulteration. Additionally, if you carry salt to the test in your pockets you risk being discovered because employees are routinely asked to open their pockets or purses.

Other Commonly Used Adulterants

In his underground classic, *Conquering The Urine Tests*, Nightbyrd describes other adulterants, such as two tablespoons of bleach or a capful of ammonia. Attempts to adulterate with ammonia is easily given away by its strong odor. When liquid bleach is added directly to urine it will oxidize and destroy THC and other cannabinoids. Using bleaches that have blue dots in them is not effective because the blue dots make it obvious that the sample has been adulterated. Alternatively, hydrogen peroxide, which is odorless, causes a chemical reaction and can alter the urine to the point where there will be a negative result.

Research has shown that Liquid Drano® will cause false negative test results for cocaine, barbiturates, amphetamines, opiates, and marijuana. However, when first put into the urine sample it bubbles and fizzes which can give the adulteration away. Another drawback is that Drano increases urine pH to

Don't Be Stupid

All of the methods of attempting to "rig" the results of urine tests—substitutions, adulteration, and dilution—entail serious risks of discovery. And "getting caught" attempting any of these techniques will be interpreted as evidence of drug use. Further, any significant chance of succeeding at such tampering requires meticulously detailed advance knowledge of the conditions and procedures of collection, as well as at least a general knowledge of the testing technology that will be used. Even a thorough effort to flush the system cannot guarantee a negative result for a drug test. Abstinence is clearly the best policy for any employee facing the possibility of a drug test who wants to keep his or her job. Drug testing labs assure employers that cheaters can be caught. They maintain that they regularly test beat-the-test products and that they do not work.

Furthermore, states are fighting back. As mentioned previously, Nebraska and Texas have enacted laws that criminalize falsifying drug test results. In 1998 a Pennsylvania law went into effect that makes it a misdemeanor to sell, share or use drug free urine to evade a positive drug test.

CHAPTER 18

You're Positive—Now What?

If your result is positive, expect to be contacted by the Medical Review Officer (MRO) for an interview to give you an opportunity to provide a "valid alternative medical explanation", such as the use of a prescripton or over-the-counter drug. Under the Federal Mandatory Guidelines a Medical Review Officer (MRO) is required to interview you before your positive result is sent to your company. This includes a review of the Custody and Control Form (CCF) for completion and accuracy.

If all of the information on the CCF appears correct and complete, no problems are noted by either the collector or the lab on the CCF, and you are unable to provide a valid alternative medical explanation, a positive lab test result is determined as "POSITIVE" and reported to your company.

If the information you submit is sufficient to support the legitimate medical use of a prescription medication that would cause the positive test result for the drug reported by the lab, the MRO can determine that result will be reported to your company as a verified "NEGATIVE". Use of medical marijuana, even with a doctor's prescription, is not an acceptable explanation. The 1998 National Drug Control Strategy says that "there is no legitimate medical explanation for a safe-sensitive worker testing positive for marijuana in the DOT or any other Federally-mandated drug-testing program."

If the MRO is unable to locate you or if you refuse to meet, the MRO will probably verify a positive test as "POSITIVE". The MRO should have documented attempts to locate and meet with you on file. So, if you get a positive result and are not contacted by the MRO, you should have your lawyer request documentation of attempts to locate you.

If as a job candidate you are told that the test was positive, you can request that the result be "confirmed" or that you be tested again. Of course, this request may be denied, because you have fewer rights before you start working. A number of companies will not administer a retest; instead they will tell you to wait six months and then reapply. By demanding a retest you make something of a big deal of it, and while you're supposed to have confidentiality, we all know that these things have a way of leaking out. If you are a recreational drug user, waiting the six months may well be the best course. Hopefully, they will have discarded your first application along with the record of the positive result. Alternatively, you might clean up your act and apply for work elsewhere.

If you are already on staff and you were tested because of an accident on the job or as part of a random testing program, the company is obligated to confirm the test result if you requested it.

Confirmatory Tests

A second test done on a sample that tested positive is called a "confirmatory test," which is more sensitive than the screening test and identifies specific drugs. To be valid, confirmatory tests must use a testing method based upon a different chemical principle from that used in the less specific screening test.

Two confirmatory methods are gas chromatography (GC) and gas chromatography/mass spectrometry (GC/MS). These methods require special instrumentation, a highly skilled operator, and a specialized lab, and are more expensive.

Ask For A Retest

Companies are legally obligated to offer you the opportunity to be retested if you are an employee (as compared to being a job applicant) and have tested positive. If the original sample was split, as is usually the case, this second test will normally be performed on the portion of the sample that was saved. To split the specimen means that the sample is split into two samples so that each can be tested separately. If split specimens were collected, the lab is required to keep both specimen bottles frozen for one year. This is generally a sufficient amount of time to allow for a retest to occur. The time, however, can be extended beyond one year to allow completion of any litigation or arbitration that may be ongoing.

The Medical Review Officer must inform you of your right to request an analysis of the split specimen. Your request to have the split specimen tested must be made through the MRO. You are normally given a maximum of 72 hours to initiate the request if you are employed at the time you get the positive test result.

What To Do

Find out if the sample was split. If the original sample was not split, a new specimen will be required. If a split sample was taken, find out if the saved portion was frozen. If it was not frozen, then it may have deteriorated. If your positive result was in fact due to your use of drugs, this deterioration is likely to be to your advantage, because it could cause a false negative. But a false negative is not guaranteed. It is something of a crap shoot. Alternatively, you can use the possibility of deterioration as a basis for insisting that the confirmatory test be taken from a fresh specimen, which gives you the opportunity to abstain and/or to flush your system in preparation for giving a new sample.

It is generally wise to exercise your right to a second test according to whichever available procedure seems most appropriate. This move buys you time and allows for the possibility of a negative result that would throw the initial positive into question, as well as being consistent with claims of innocence. In fact, if you claim to be innocent you may garner suspicion by *not* insisting upon a second test.

Prescribed Drugs

The Federal Guidelines require the MRO to verify a drug test result as a negative result if you have a legitimate alternative medical explanation, such as having a prescription. Don't be surprised if the MRO asks for the name of the prescribing physician to discuss the possible impact that the medication you are taking may have upon your work. If you have a medical condition, the American Disabilities Act (ADA) has placed restrictions on what questions the MRO can ask and what can be done with that information.

Testing Positive For Prescribed Drugs

When you have no prescription, otherwise legal drugs become contraband and are treated as illegal drugs. But disciplining you for legally prescribed drugs is unfair and prohibited under the American Disabilities Act. For one thing, you have done nothing wrong except, perhaps, failing to inform the company about the medical circumstance in question. In most cases, you are not required to inform your company of legitimate medicines you're taking. That's your private business.

Discipline is permitted*only* if the company policy refers specifically to legally prescribed drugs and requires disclosure of such use. However, such a policy may be illegal under the ADA. A lawyer can help you with this. You might even be able to get one on contigency, because violations of the ADA carry big monetary penalties.

Your employer is not permitted to go on a fishing trip looking for prescribed medicines you might be taking and trying to uncover ailments. This is strictly against the law. If this happens, you probably have grounds for a lawsuit.

The ADA has thrown sand into the drug testing system. For example, when you apply for a job, drug testing is permitted but testing for alcohol is not, because alcoholism is considered a disability and alcohol testing is considered a medical examination. Medical examinations of disabled people applying for a job are prohibited. Here's the crazy thing: drug addiction is considered a disability provided you have been rehabilitated or are in rehabilitation. Employers are not permitted to probe into any disabilities you might have during a job interview. This means that an employer cannot ask you if you are a drug addict or if you used drugs in the past. The employer can ask you if you currently use drugs, because current use is considered illegal use whereas past use is probing into a possbile disability.

If you have a disability it is illegal to single you out for drug testing. You can, however, be tested, as long as you are in no way treated differently because of your disability. If you have been in a drug rehab program, you are considered disabled and this information cannot be used in considering you for a job. The company is not permitted to ask you about your disability, including drug addiction. On the other hand, you can be grilled on your current use, which is illegal and fair game. In this morass of confusion and contradictory rules are loopholes you might be able to use if you get a positive drug test and can claim to have a drug abuse disability.

Confidentiality

Insist upon confidentiality. Your test results should not be given out to anyone while you are attempting to have the matter resolved and, preferably, expunged from the record. You or your attorney can submit a written notice requesting confidentiality, or you can request a letter from your union. It is wise to send such a request by certified mail or another delivery method that produces documentation that it has been received.

In most states, all medical records are protected under legal standards of privacy, and employers are required to take necessary steps to ensure confidentiality of employees' records. In these states, revealing test results to third parties is an infringement of your rights. However, never assume that confidentiality is automatic.

Maintain A Paper Trail

Keep copies of all relevant documents. Memoranda of important conversations with your supervisor or other company officials should be written and filed in a log or diary that includes notes on times, places, and names. Ask that all requests from your company and determinations be given to you in writing.

Under the whistle-blowing laws, it is illegal for you to be fired for challenging the test results. But of course it can still happen. Maintaining a "paper trail" ensures that you will be able to convincingly reconstruct events in case you have to defend against discipline, such as termination.

CHAPTER 19

Your Company Must Be Fair

How an employer handles a positive test result depends on a variety of factors, including the nature of the job, your past employment record, whether the drug use took place on the job, and the perceived severity of your so-called drug abuse problem. If there is other evidence that you were under the influence while on the job, you are more likely to be terminated than if your drug usage was not job-related.

What you do off the job is usually of no consequence or concern to the company. There are plenty of exceptions, however. If the employer can show a relationship between your off-duty behavior and the job, then disciplinary action is pretty likely. Nonetheless, even with illegal off-duty behavior, it is the employer's burden to establish a link between that misconduct and job performance, and this can be difficult to prove. Often a company has covered itself for this eventuality by adding drug-free conditions to the company policy statement. The argument is that you have agreed to be drug-free because you read the policy and then accepted the job with all of the conditions—as defined by the company policy—that come with it. This type of argument has been upheld by the Courts, who have bought the argument that drug testing is "voluntary" because it is in the company policy. It's like volunteering when you have a gun to your head!

The Particular Problem Of Marijuana

Marijuana presents several unique problems. Marijuana use is illegal, but in many jurisdictions its use or possession is no more serious than a traffic ticket. It is the most-used illegal drug in our country, particularly among younger people. In general, its use is not considered as serious as the use of cocaine, LSD, or so-called "hard drugs" such as heroin and methedrine. In the late 1990s several counties passed voter initiatives legalizing medical marijuana, further confusing the issue.

This ambivalence toward marijuana has manifested in arbitration decisions. Some arbitrators will sustain discharges for simple marijuana use on company premises, and others will not. The case for discharge is stronger when several incidents of usage occur, however, or when a large quantity is found in the your possession, which will be used to build a case that you are a dope dealer.

Another complication is that marijuana traces appear in urine for days—even weeks—after use. A lot of folks live in communities that have relaxed attitudes towards smoking dope, yet you can be treated like a criminal if you get a positive drug test for pot. Cannabis metabolites are stored in the fat cells for long periods of time. The positive result could be indicating usage several days or even weeks in the past, and may not be correlated with impairment of job performance.

Passive Inhalation

Another major problem with drug testing for cannabinoids is that you can test positive even if you didn't inhale. Research has demonstrated that people who were present while marijuana was smoked by others tested positive, even though they did not smoke any themselves.

In a NIDA study, Dr. Cone demonstrated that THC, the psychoactive component in marijuana, accumulates fasters in the fatty tissues of people passively inhaling the smoke than in the person actually smoking! Further, the greater your body fat, the longer the detection time. Cone documented detection times up to 9 days following exposure to passive, second hand marijuana smoke. Clearly, an employer has no right to discipline you for the behavior of your friends or to dictate where you can go for recreation and entertainment, if it is otherwise lawful. If you are disciplined or discharged for "dirty" urine under these circumstances you might be able to bring a lawsuit based on the torts of intrusion or defamation.

Employers Must Follow Procedures

An employer who suspects you of drug use is expected to act reasonably in accordance with the company's stated personnel policy and your work record. The employer must follow the company's termination procedures. Employers are accorded particularly wide latitude if health or safety is at risk. Since drug and alcohol use is commonly linked to accidents, mishaps, and other incidents involving breach of safety, employers will have more freedom to discipline you if the affected job involves safety risk to co-workers or the public, such as jobs related to public utilities or transport, or involving machinery. Regardless, employers are still expected to treat you fairly.

Fairness

An employer is required to handle any termination for drug- or alcohol-related offenses in the same reasonable manner as other terminations. The Federal Mandatory Guidelines require that the MRO review the facts for objectivity and to ensure that proper procedures have been consistently followed.

Your company should be consistent in procedures and practices. If you've gotten a positive drug test, you should request a written statement of the drug testing policy and the procedures for handling positive results. Be alert for mistakes and inconsistencies in the way that you are treated. These may provide handles for your attorney if you end up in litigation. You should be provided with a full opportunity to express your side.

Progressive Discipline

"Employment-at-will" allows your employer to fire you whether or not there is a valid reason. If you work in the private sector, an employment-at-will situation may exist if there is no union or other employment agreement regarding termination procedures. However, many Courts now give a discharged employee grounds for suit against an employer if the discharge is in bad faith, abusive, wrongful, or against public policy.

Generally the company's personnel manual or policy statement is viewed as constituting an implicit employment contract or as superceding a signed contract which provided for discipline-at-will. Consequently, even in an employment-at-will situation, the company policy and procedure should accurately state the consequences of urine testing, and these policies and company procedures should be followed.

Gather together your employment contract (if you have one), the personnel manual and any other memos the company issued concerning the drug testing program. Keep a written record of how you are treated. If your lawyer can show that your treatment was unfair and did not follow the company's stated guidlines, you may be able to beat the rap.

Arbitrator Review

Labor agreements typically require that all discharges be reviewed by an arbitrator, who will look at several issues. First, the arbitrator will decide whether the employer's description of the situation is accurate. Was the test accurate enough to prove the use of the drug? Was the chain of custody of the sample clear? Was the test performed properly?

Second, the arbitrator will decide whether you violated a company rule or the terms of the labor agreement. In the absence of clear rules, the arbitrator may overturn the discharge on the basis that you lacked fair notice of the consequences of getting a positive drug test.

Third, the arbitrator will decide whether the sanctions imposed are fair and equitable, or too harsh. An arbitrator who feels the sanctions are too harsh is empowered to reverse the sanction in favor of a lesser penalty. Here is where questions concerning off-the-job conduct, your past record, severity of the conduct and other relevant information will be considered. The arbitrator may ask if progressive disciplinary actions were applied, and, if not, why not. Under labor agreements, compensation is generally limited to orders of reinstatement and back pay, whereas in the employment-at-will situation, damages may be awarded for categories such as mental anguish.

Termination

If there is any doubt about whether you were informed regarding policies requiring submission of urine samples, or about negative consequences for refusal to give a sample, the arbitrator is likely to resolve the issue in your favor, especially when your job is at stake. The loophole is demonstrating that the company policy and personnel handbook neglected to clearly inform you of expectations regarding drug use and drug testing, or that such official company documents were too vague. The rule of thumb is that the company should inform you in advance of the details concerning when urine samples may be requested and the consequences of refusal.

CHAPTER 20

What About A Leave Of Absence?

Another law that might provide you with a legal loophole is the Family and Medical Leave Act (FMLA), enacted in 1993. FMLA requires your company to give you an unpaid leave of absence where you are entitled to return to your job or an "equivalent" job. This can sound mighty good if you're facing a stint in rehab which means you're going to be away from the job. You can go clean up and hopefully get it together, and have the security of returning to your job.

The catch is that you must qualify. FMLA is a Federal regulation, so you know up front that there are a lot of particular conditions. But if you can qualify, FMLA could help you keep your life together after the catastrophe of a positive drug test.

Does Your Company Qualify?

Both you and your company must meet certain requirements to come under the FMLA provisions. You must work for a private employer with 50 or more employees, working within a 75-mile radius. The 50 or more employees have to have worked each working day, during each of 20 or more calendar workweeks in the current or preceding calendar year.

Leave Requirements

If your company meets the FMLA requirements it must provide leaves of absences to eligible employees. If you qualify, you are entitled to 12 workweeks of unpaid family and medical leave per year. You can take it all at once, or you can break it into segments. When the leave is over, you are entitled (in most cases) to return to your job or an equivalent job—in terms of benefits, pay and other terms and conditions of employment.

Are You Eligible For FMLA Leave

Once again, to be eligible your company must itself qualify and you must meet certain Federal requirements pertaining to the length of your employment with the company and the reason for the leave.

Length of Employment

You must have worked for your company, which itself must meet the regulation terms, for at least 12 months—which can be sequential or cumulative. If you are a part-time or seasonal worker, you can still qualify provided you have worked at least 1,250 hours in the preceding 12 months, which is around 24 hours a week as a minimum.

Reason For Taking A Leave

Your reason for taking time off from work must be to care for a "serious health condition"—yours or that of your child, spouse or parent. A serious health condition is defined by the Feds as an illness, injury, impairment, or physical or mental condition that involves inpatient care or continuing treatment which includes a period of incapacity. Incapacity is further defined in the law. If you think you might qualify for FMLA, you'll need to review the definitions with an advocate (lawyer, counselor, etc.) who is schooled in this law.

Certificate

Most employers will require certification of your condition from a healthcare provider verifying that you or your family member has a serious health conditions that requires inpatient care and/or continuous treatment. The Department of Labor makes a model certification form available to employers, and perhaps you can get one. Basically, it is like a letter from your doctor.

Not A Shield From Discipline

Getting a FMLA leave does not get you off the hook with your employers, however. Your company can still take so-called disciplinary action against you if you violated the company drug-free workplace policy. It seems kind of useless to go through all the hassle of getting an official leave of absence that guarantees your job back, only to be fired anyway and have no job to come back to.

Well, if you've gotten yourself into this situation, you're dealing with Federal laws. The Feds want to make sure no so-called recreational user slips though under the label of drug addict! But take heart, there is a loophole, Maybe you can wiggle through it.

First off, the company cannot take adverse action against you because you exercise your right to FMLA leave for treatment. So if you think you qualify, don't hesitate to "exercise your right".

Second, the company can take action against you only if there is an established drug-free workplace policy that is applied in a nondiscriminatory manner, that has been communicated to all employees, and that clearly spells out when you can be terminated. There are potential loopholes in each of the previous phrases. If there is no "established policy", if you can show the policy is used to discriminate, if you can show that it wasn't clearly communicated, or if the policy is not clear as to when you can be terminated, then legally they can't fire you and you are entitled to a FMLA leave of absence. Phew!

CHAPTER 21

Challenging The Results

The first line of defense when you get a positive result is to get it confirmed. If the positive is confirmed, the next defense is to challenge the test and its results. You might challenge the reason that the test was given, you might challenge the method of confirmation and other procedures or you might assert that the positive was caused by cross-reactivity.

Probable Cause

The Fourth Amendment to the Constitution prevents the government from invading the privacy of citizens. For example, it prohibits search and seizure in the absence of "probable cause." The Fifth Amendment prohibits the government from requiring that you testify in a self-incrimatory manner. These amendments restrict the actions that the government can take not only toward the citizenry at large but also toward its own employees. Thus, government employees have special protections in regard to their employer and employment that are not necessarily available to employees of private companies. For instance, "probable cause" must theoretically be present for a drug test—which is considered a form of search and seizure—

to be performed. Thus, if you are a government employee your lawyer might challenge the test on the basis that there was no probable cause—or good reason—for giving *you* the test. Such challenges have succeeded, but they've generally involved groups of plaintiffs. A single person trying to bring a constitutional defense, especially if he or she is part of random testing, is in for a long and expensive haul.

Union members who test positive should seek help from their union. Unions have proven effective and successful in carrying through legal proceedings to defend their members against unfair treatment in drug testing situations.

The Cross-Reactivity Challenge

Results can be challenged on the basis of cross-reactivity. You claim that another substance, such as an over-the-counter medication or a legally obtained prescription, was taken and caused the positive result. The company will probably insist upon a second, more sophisticated confirmatory test which is less vulnerable to cross-reactivity, and its results will be interpreted as conclusive. The confirmatory test is likley to be performed upon the original urine specimen. However, if for whatever reason a fresh sample is to be used, you'd be wise to cease using any illegal or over-the-counter substances immediately in the hope of clearing your system before the confirmatory test.

Challenging The Confirmatory Method

If you can demonstrate that your urinalysis test result was not properly confirmed or that the test was improperly performed, you might be able to bring a negligence action against your employer. The basis of such an action is that the person conducting the test and the employer who ordered the test have a legal duty to see that the manufacturer's directions are properly followed and that the screening test is confirmed in a proper manner. Failure to fulfill this duty, and subsequent harm caused to you by loss of work or by other disciplinary actions, can be the basis for a lawsuit.

Challenging Procedures

Any step in the drug testing procedure can be challenged, including the chain of custody, the monitoring procedures, and so forth. The assistance of an attorney or a union are usually needed for such challenges.

Chain Of Custody

"Chain of custody" is a monitoring process to prevent tampering with the sample or the results. Chain of custody begins with collection of the urine and continues through the final reporting of test results to clients. Sealing of sample containers, transport and control of samples, receipt of samples by the laboratory, and supervision of lab tests remain under strict discipline throughout the chain of custody. Authorized signatures are required at each step. Laboratory results can be effectively challenged in court if there are weak links in the chain.

Standards regulate the handling, analysis, and collection of samples if they are intended to be admissible in a Court of law. Transfer of urine, blood, or saliva from the subject to the container must be witnessed. For example, if a person is taken to a physician for a blood sample, the physician becomes the first link in the chain of custody. Few physicians understand the legal chain of custody procedures. Unless otherwise instructed, they will usually follow clinical laboratory standards, which will not stand up to challenge by a knowledgeable attorney.

The person collecting the blood sample must be able to testify regarding the collection procedure. Likewise, the person collecting the sample must be able to testify to the accuracy of the container label, including the subject's name and other identifying information, such as date, time of the collection, and type of collection receptacle. The chain of custody must be maintained until the specimen reaches the laboratory—and through the confirmation of intitial results.

Fatal Flaws

The following errors or omissions in the documentation for a sample are considered fatal flaws that result in a specimen being rejected for testing by the lab. 1) The preprinted specimen I.D. number on the CCF does not match the specimen I.D. number on the specimen bottle. 2) There is no specimen I.D. number on the bottle. 3) There is an insufficient quantity of urine for the lab to complete the test. 4) The specimen bottle label and or seal is mssing, broken, or shows evidence of tampering. 5) The specimen bottle is obviously adulterated—color, foreign objects, unusual odor. Other errors or omissions may be fatal flaws unless the information can be recovered or provided in writing by the collector to the lab.

CHAPTER 22

Should You Sue?

If you have a confirmed positive test and don't claim to be disabled by drug addiction, you may well face termination. When threatened with termination the assistance of the union or an attorney is essential. Stopping the termination is easier than attempting to become reinstated.

A lawsuit against an employer is usually based on the grounds of wrongful discharge, infliction of mental stress and perhaps slander and defamation if the employer violated the confidentiality of your records. Establishing grounds for these challenges are very difficult.

Wrongful discharge cases are ordinarily hard to win. However, according to attorney Patrick Bishop, publisher of *Criminal Law Monthly,* the attorney should be able to convince the judge to have the employer disclose all the documents pertaining to the test results. This disclosure provides the attoney with the opportunity to research these documents in search of violations of the forensic standards in sample collection or in the types of tests used, or to expose some other kind of flaw in the testing procedures. Attorneys Edward Chen of the Northern California American Civil Liberties Union and John True of the San Francisco Employment Law Center have outlined several innovative defenses using common-law theory and other torts in an article entitled, "Recent Developments in Employee Drug Testing."

Pros and Cons of Suing

Whether or not you should sue for reinstatement or for damages is another consideration. It is usually easier to retain an attorney when monetary damages are demanded, rather than only reinstatement and back pay, because such damages, if awarded, can provide you with the means of paying the attorney.

Some employees have been successful in legal challenges after years in the process. A San Francisco jury awarded $485,042 to a woman fired from her computer programming job with Southern Pacific Railroad because she refused to submit to urinalysis (*Luck* v. *Southern Pacific Transportation Company*). The New York Supreme Court ruled that mandatory testing of public school teachers is unconstitutional (*Patchogue-Medford Congress of Teachers* v. *The Board of Education*). In San Francisco, a Federal Court found that train operators could not be tested simply because they had been in an accident. The Court ruled that the employer must have a "particularized suspicion" that the employee was under the influence of drugs or alcohol while on the job (*Railroad Executives Association* v. *Burnley*).

The Stress Of Suing

The repercussions of a lawsuit can be felt well beyond the current employment situation. The stigma which results may attach itself not only to you, but to your spouse and children as well when friends and neighbors hear about the lawsuit and suspect that you are really a druggie trying to beat the rap.

The process of a lawsuit is expensive and stressful. In Court, the employer's attorney will try to make you appear to be a drug addict. Private eyes are often hired to snoop into your personal life and dig up dirt on you. You may find yourself defending a weekend binge from your college days, for example, when you may have experimented with drugs or had friends who were drug users.

Request Rehabilitation

Instead of a legal challenge you could cop a plea and ask for the chance to "rehabilitate" yourself. This may sound obnoxious, especially if you do not consider yourself to be disabled. But having a disability offers protection under the American Disabilities Act. And let's face it, your job is on the line. If you lose your job, then what? What are you going give as a reason when applying for a new job? It sucks, but it is a loophole that may be worth going for.

Once you claim to be an addict, then direct disciplinary action or termination is less likely. Technically, only past drug abuse is considered a disability whereas current use—which is what is detected by a drug test—is considered illegal behavior and not a disability. But the distinction between current and past is murky and the penalties to employers who volate the ADA is high. When you claim to be an addict, the company is then required to offer you the opportunity of rehabilitation and you will be referred to approved treatment, such as counseling or intensive drug rehabilitation therapy. If you fail to work conscientiously toward recovery and to cooperate with therapy, then you can be disciplined or terminated.

Another approach is to argue that your drug use was casual and that you can and *will* stop. To show your commitment and resolve, you can request the opportunity to demonstrate it by submitting to regular testing and which you promise will yield negative results. If your positive result was for pot and you work in a progressive area that has a more permissive attitude about dope, you might succeed. But then you must contend with more testing—which probably means abstinence.

Unemployment Benefits

Collecting unemployment benefits after being fired for refusing to take a drug test or for getting a positive result is so difficult as to be considered impossible. The relevant regulations vary from state to state. The California Unemployment Compensation Appeals Board has ruled that employees in hazardous jobs who are fired for refusing to submit to drug tests based on a reasonable suspicion of drug use are not entitled to benefits. In contrast, in Oregon, an Appellate Court ruled that an employee fired after testing positive for drug use is entitled to unemployment benefits since the test results alone do not show that the employee was fired for work-related conduct. The trend is for increased restrictiveness. In 1998 four states—Virginia, Colorado, Tennessee and Mississippi—passed bills limiting unemployment benefits. Employees who contemplate refusing to be tested or who worry they may get a positive result would be wise to make inquiries to the unemployment compensation departments in their respective states before testing.

Prepare In Advance

Preparing in advance is the best course. Do what you can reasonably do to prevent getting a positive result in the first place. The best protection is to stop using all drugs, including alcohol, over-the-counter, and prescription drugs in preparation for the test. Employees and athletes who have serious health problems should never stop taking their medication because of a pending drug test, however. In the case of prescription drugs, it is best to consult a physican.

BIBLIOGRAPHY

American Civil Liberties Union, What ACLU Has to Say About Drug Testing in the Workplace, American Civil Liberties Union, New York, 1986.

Baselt, R. C., Stability of Cocaine in Biological Fluids, *Journal of Chromatography*, 1983, vol. 268, no. 3, pp. 502-505.

Baumgartner, W. A., V. A. Hill, and W. H. Blahd, Hair Analysis for Drugs of Abuse, *Journal of Forensic Science*, 1989, vol. 34, pp. 1433-1453.

Berger, Gilda, *Drug Testing*, Impact Books, NY, 1987.

Blanck, D. L., and D. A. Kidwell, External Contamination of Hair by Cocaine: An Issue In Forensic Interpretation, *Forensic Science International*, 1993, vol. 63, pp. 145-156.

Bogdanich, Walt, Labs Offering Workplace Drug Screens in New York Have Higher Error Rate, *The Wall Street Journal*, Feb. 2, 1987.

Bogdanich, Walt, Medical Labs, Trusted as Largely Error-Free, are Far From Infallible, *The Wall Street Journal*, Feb. 2, 1987.

Boone, Joe, *Obtaining and Maintaining Reliable Drug Testing Services*, Centers for Disease Control, Public Health Service, U.S. Dept. of Health and Human Services, pp. 1-8.

Cais, M., S. Dani, and M. Shimoni, A Novel Non-Centrifugation Radioimmunoassay for Cannabinoids, *Isr. Arch. Toxicology*, 1983, vol. 53, suppl. 6, pp. 105-113.

California Government Code, Dept. of Personnel Administration, Title 2, Article 29, Substance Abuse, Sep. 16, 1989, reg. 89, no. 37.

California Government Code, State Personnel Board, Title 2, 213, May 6, 1989, reg. 89, no. 18.

Carlseen, William, Trucker Fights "Zero Tolerance" Seizure of Rig, *San Francisco Chronicle*, Jul. 1988.

Center for Disease Control, The Results of Unregulated Testing, JAMA, Apr. 26, 1985.

Chen, Edward, and John M. Ture, III, Recent Developments in Employment Drug Testing, *Civil Rights and Attorney's Fee Annual Handbook*, 1989, vol. 4.

Cody, J. T. and R. H. Schwarzhoff, Impact of Adulterants of RIA Analysis of Urine for Drugs of Abuse, *Journal of Analytical Toxicology*, 1989, vol. 13, pp. 277-284.

Collins, Robert, U. S. District Judge, Perspectives Quote, *Newsweek*, Nov. 24, 1986, pp. 29.

Cone, E. J., et al., Passive Inhalation of Marijuana Smoke: Urinalysis and Room Air Levels of Delta-9-Tetrahydrocannabinol, *Journal of Analytical Toxicology*, 1987, 11, pp. 89-96.

Cone, E. J., Marijuana Effects and Urinalysis After Passive Inhalation and Oral Ingestion. Laboratory of Chemical and Drug Metabolism, NIDA, *Research Monograph*, 1990, vol. 99, pp. 88-96.

Cone, E. J., R.E. Johnson, W. D. Darwin, D. Yousefnejad, L.D. Mell, B. D. Paul, and J. Mithcell, Passive Inhalation of Marijuana Smoke: Urinalysis and Room Levels of Delta-9-Tetrahydrocannabinol, *Journal of Analytical Toxicology*, 1987, vol. 11, pp. 89-95.

Cone, E. J., Testing human hair for drugs of abuse: Individual does and time profiles of morphine and codeine in plasma, saliva, urine, and beard compared to drug-induced effects on pupils and behavior, *Journal of American Toxicology*, 1990, 14, pp. 1-7.

Cone, E.J., M.J. Hillsgrove, A.J. Jenkins, R. M. Keenan, and W.D. Darwin, Sweat testing for heroin, cocaine, and metabolites, *Journal of Analytical Toxicology*, 1994, 18, pp. 298-305.

Crane, Richard, Legal Issues in Employee Drug Detection Programs, Syva Product Literature, Syva Co., Palo Alto, CA., 1987.

de Bernardo, Mark A., and Nancy N. Delogu, *1997-1998 Guide to State and Federal Drug-Testing Laws, Sixth Edition, Institute for a Drug-Free Workplace* (800/842-7400), Washington, D.C.

de Bernardo, Mark A., *Drug & Alcohol Abuse Prevention and the ADA: An Employer's Guide*, The Institute for a Drug-Free Workplace, Washington D.C., 1992.

Decresce, Robert P., and Mark S. Lifshits, *Drug Testing in The Workplace*, American Society of Clinical Pathologists Press and The Bureau of National Affairs Books, 1989.

Dutt, M. C., Laboratory Diagnosis of Opiate Drugs, Ann. Acad. *Med. Singapore*, 1984, vol. 13, no. 1, pp. 53-65.

Elahi, Nasik, Encapsulated XAD-2 Extraction Technique for a Rapid Screening of Drugs of Abuse in Urine, *Journal Analytical Toxicology, Jan./Feb. 1980*, vol. 4, pp. 26-30.

Ferslew, K. E., J. E. Manno, and B. R. Manno, Determination of Urinary Cannabinoid Metabolites Following Incidental Exposure to Marijuana Smoke, *Res. Common Substance Abuse*, 1983, vol. 4, no. 4, pp. 289-300.

Freeman, Robert, How to "Beat" a Drug Test, High Times, Aug. 1988, no. 156, pp. 19.

Gieringer, Dale, (ed.) Drug Testing Advice, California *NORMAL Reports*, Feb. 1988, vol. 12, no. 1.

Goldberg, Jeff, and Dean Latimer, Future Drugs - They're All in Your Head, High Times, Oct. 1987.

Gottheil, Edward, Glenn R. Caddy, Ph.D., and Deborah L. Austin, Fallibility of Urine Drug Screens in Monitoring Methadone Programs, *JAMA*, Aug. 30, 1976, vol. 236, no. 9, pp. 1035-1038.

Guinn, Bobby, Job Satisfaction, Counterproductive Behavior and Circumstantial Drug Use Among Long-Distance Truckers, *Journal of Psychoactive Drugs*, Jul./Sep. 1983, vol. 15, no. 3, pp. 185-188.

Gupta, R. N., Drug Level Monitoring: Sedative Hypnotics, *Journal of Chromatography Biomedical Application*, 1986, vol. 340, pp. 139-172.

Hanners, David, Powdered Urine Seen as Million Dollar Idea, *The Dallas Morning News*, Dec. 14, 1986.

Henderson, G. L., M.R. Harkey, and C. Zhou, Incorporation of Isotopically Labeled Cocaine and Metabolites Into Human Hair: 1 Dose-Response Relationships, *Journal of Analytical Toxicology*, 1996, vol. 20, pp. 1-11.

Herzfeld, John, Brain Scans on the Job?, American Health, Jul./Aug. 1986, pp. 72.

Hoffman, Abbie, with Jonathan Silvers, *Steal This Urine Test*, Penguin Books, 1987.

Hoffman, Joan W., and Ken Jennings, Will Drug Testing in Sports Play for Industry? *Personnel Journal*, May 1987, pp. 52.

Holtorf, Kent, *UR-INE Trouble*, Vandalay Press, Scottsdale, 1997.

Jenkins, A.J., R.M. Keenan, J.E. Henningfield, and E. J. Cone, Pharmacokinestics and pharmocodynamics of smoking heroin, *Journal of Analytical Toxicology*, 1994, 18, pp. 317-330.

Jones, A. B., H. N. Elsohly, E. S. Aragat, and M. A. ElSohly, Analysis of the Major Metabolite of Delta-9 Tetrahydrocannabinol in Urine, IV, A Comparison of Five Methods, *Journal Analytical Toxicology*, 1984, vol. 8, no. 6, pp. 249-251.

Jones, Donald W., D. Adams, P. Martel, and R. Rousseau, Drug Population in 1000 Geographically Distributed Urine Specimens, *Journal Analytical Toxicology*, May/Jun. 1985, vol. 9, pp. 125-130.

Joseph, R. E., T. Su, and E. J. Cone, In Vitro Binding Studies of Drugs Into Hair: Influence of Melanin and Lipids on Cocaine Binding to Causasoid and Africoid Hair, *Journal of Analytical Toxicology*, 1996, vol. 20, pp. 338-344.

Joseph, R., S. Dickerson, R. Willis, D. Frankenfield, E. J. Cone, and D. R. Smith, *Interference by Nonsteroidal Anti-Inflammatory Drugs in EMIT and TDx Assays for Drugs of Abuse*, 1995, vol. 19, pp. 13-17.

Kim, Hyum J., and Eugene Cerceo, Interference by NaCl With the EMIT Method of Analysis for Drugs of Abuse, *Clinical Chemistry*, 1976, vol. 22, no. 11, pp. 1935.

Klein, Alfred, Employees Under the Influence - Outside the Law?, *Personnel Journal*, Sep. 1986, pp. 57-71.

Klein, Joe, The New Drug They Call Ecstasy, *This World*, Jun. 23, 1985, pp. 10-11.

Latimer, Dean, "Freedom Chemist" Admits Scam: "Melanin", High Times, Apr. 1987, pp. 20.

Latimer, Dean, Drug Test Shocker: Alka Seltzer Scores as Dope!, High T*imes*, Sep. 1986, pp. 15.

Latimer, Dean, Highwitness News: What To Do If You're Fired By A. Urine Test, *High Times, Nov. 1986*, pp. 14.

Latimer, Dean, Reliability of Drug Tests, *High Times*, Oct. 1986, pp. 56-59.

Law, B., P. A. Mason, A. C. Moffat, and L. J. King, A Novel 125-I Radioimmunoassay for the Analysis of Delta-9 Tetrahydrcannabinal and its Metabolites in Human Body Fluids, *Journal Analytical Toxicology*, 1984, vol. 8, no. 1, pp. 14-18.

Law, B., P. A. Mason, A. C. Moffat, and L. J. King, Confirmation of Cannabis Use by the Analysis of Delta-9 Tetrahydrocannibinol Metabolites in Blood and Urine by Combined HPLC and RIA, *Journal Analytical Toxicology*, 1984, vol. 8, no. 1, pp. 19-22.

Law, B., P. A. Mason, and A. C. Moffat, Forensic Aspects of the Metabolism and Excretion of Cannabinoids Following Oral Ingestion of Cannabis Resin, *Journal Pharmaceutical Pharmacology*, 1984, vol. 36, no. 5, pp. 289-294.

Lora-Tamayo, C., T. Tena, and A. Rodriguez, High concentration of Ciprofloxacin in Urine Invalidates EMIT Results, *Journal of Analytical Toxicology*, 1966, vol. 20, pp. 334.

Lurie, I. S., Problems in Using High Performance Liquid Chromatography for Drug Analysis, *Journal Forensic Science*, 1984, vol. 8, no. 6, pp. 149-251.

McBurney, L. J., B. A. Bobbie, and L. A. Sepp, GC/Ms and EMIT Analysis for Delta 9-Tetrahydrocannabinol Metabolites in Plasma and Urine of Human Subjects, *Journal Analytical Toxicology*, Mar./Apr. 1986, vol. 10, pp. 56-64.

McCarron, Margaret M., Phencyclidine Intoxication, *PharmChem Newsletter*, May/Jun. 1986, vol. 15, no. 3, pp. 1-8.

Mikkelsen, S. L., and K. O. Ash, Adulterants Causing False Negatives in Illicit Drug Testing, *Clinical Chemistry*, 1988, vol. 34, pp. 2333-2336.

Montague, Mary W., Bosses Strike Back a Sample-Salting, High Times, Oct. 1986, pp. 15.

Morgan, M.D., John P., Problems of Mass Urine Screening for Misused Drugs, *Substance Abuse in the Workplace,* Haight Ashbury Publications, San Francisco, 1984, pp. 21.

National Drug Control Strategy, U.S. Government Printing Office, Sep. 1989.

Nightbyrd, Jeffrey, *Conquering The Urine Tests: A Complete Guide To Success in Urine Testing,* Byrd Labratories, 225 Congress, Box 340, Austin, TX 78701, 1986.

NORMAL, Urine Testing for Marijuana & Other Drugs, Common Sense for *America,* 1986, pp. 30-31.

Parker, E. Parker, J. Brody, and R. Schoenberg., Alcohol Use and Cognitive Loss Among Employed Men and Women, *AJPH,* 1983, vol. 73, pp. 521-526.

Product Brochure, PharmChem Laboratories Inc., Menlo Park, CA.

Product Literature, Abuscreen - Radioimmunoassay for Cannabinoids, Roche Diagnostic Systems, New Jersey.

Product Literature, Abuscreen - Radioimmunoassay for Morphine, Roche Dianostic Systems, New Jersey.

Product Literature, KDI Quik Test, Brown Boxenbaum, Inc., New York, Dec. 4, 1987.

Product Literature, Luckey Laboratories, Inc., San Bernardino, CA, no. S69.

Product Literature, Spot THC Without Instrumentation - Toxi-Lab Cannabinoid (THC) Screen, Analytical Systems, Kansas City, MO.

Rajananda, V., N. K. Nair, and V. Navaratnam, An Evaluation of TLC Systems for Opiate Analysis, *Bulletin of Narcotics,* 1985, vol. 37, no. 1, pp. 35-47.

Rutkowski and Associates, *Employment Law Update, Sep. 1986,* vol. 1, no. 1, pp. 1-8.

San Francisco City. Part II, Chapter VIII, Article 33A. San Francisco Municipal Code.

Schwarzhoff, R. H., and J. T. Cody, The Effect of Adulterating Agents on FPIA Analysis of Urine for Drugs of Abuse, *Journal of Analytical Toxicology,* 1993, vol. 17, pp. 14-17.

Smith, R. M., Arylhydroxy Metabolites of Cocaine in the Urine of Cocaine Users, *Journal Analytical Toxicology,* 1984, vol. 8, no. 1, pp. 35-37.

Stafford, D. T., H. S. Nichols, and W. H. Anderson, Efficiency of Capillary Column Gas Chromatography in Separating Lysergic Acid Diethylamide (LSD) and Lysergic Acid Methlypropylamide (LAMPA), *Journal Forensic Science,* 1984, vol. 29, no. 1, pp. 291-298.

Sutheimer, C. A., R. Yarborough, B. R. Hepler, and I. Sunshine, Detection and Confirmation of Urinary Cannabinoids, *Journal Analytical Toxicology,* Jul./Aug. 1985, vol. 9, pp. 156-160.

United States, The Bill of Rights, American Civil Liberties Union, Sacramento, CA.

Urine Specimen Collection Handbook for Federal Workplace Drug Testing Program, CSAP Technical Report 12, DHHS Publications No (SMA) 96-3114, 1996.

Vereby, K., D. Jukofsky, and S. J. Mule, Evaluation of a New TLC Confirmation Technique for Positive EMIT Cannabinoid Urine Samples, *Res. Common. Substance Abuse,* 1985, vol. 6, no. 1, pp. 1-9.

Vogle, Walter F., and Donna M. Bush, Medical Review Officer Manual for Federal Workplace Drug Testing Programs, Substance Abuse and Mental Health Services Administration (SAMHSA), CSAP Technical Report 15, DHHS Publication no. (SMA) 97-3164, 1997.

Index

U

V

W

Y

The Authors

Beverly A. Potter, Ph.D., earned her doctorate in counseling psychology from Stanford University and her masters in vocational rehabilitation counseling from San Francisco State.

Dr. Potter has had a wide range of experience with law enforcement, the criminal justice system, corporations, associations and colleges. She has trained police officers in "crisis intervention" and has been "on the beat". She has seen the problems of substance abuse first hand. As a researcher, she lived on a heroin treatment ward as a "participant observer" and she worked with inmates in the San Francisco County Jail.

Dr. Potter is a specialist in management psychology and has provided training for Hewlett-Packard, GTE, SUN, Becton-Dickinson, IRS, Stanford Medical School, Stanford University Staff Development, Design Management Institute, Department of Energy and others. She is the author of several books.

J. Sebastian Orfali, M.A., earned his masters degree in philosophy from the University of New Mexico. As publisher of And/Or Press and Ronin Publishing, he published over 150 books about controlled substances, health, technology and current issues, including *The Cocaine Handbook, Controlled Substanced: A Chemical And Legal Guide To The Federal Drug Laws, The Holistic Health Handbook, Secrets Of Life Extension, The Psychedelic Encyclopedia.*